New Dad Playbook to Win at Parenting

What to Expect and How to Prepare, From Conception to Six Months

Ryan Martin

© **Copyright 2022 - All rights reserved.**

The content contained within this book may not be reproduced, duplicated or transmitted without direct written permission from the author or the publisher.

Under no circumstances will any blame or legal responsibility be held against the publisher, or author, for any damages, reparation, or monetary loss due to the information contained within this book, either directly or indirectly.

Legal Notice:

This book is copyright protected. It is only for personal use. You cannot amend, distribute, sell, use, quote or paraphrase any part, or the content within this book, without the consent of the author or publisher.

Disclaimer Notice:

Please note the information contained within this document is for educational and entertainment purposes only. All effort has been executed to present accurate, up to date, reliable, complete information. No warranties of any kind are declared or implied. Readers acknowledge that the author is not engaged in the rendering of legal, financial, medical or professional advice. The content within this book has been derived from various sources. Please consult a licensed professional before attempting any techniques outlined in this book.

By reading this document, the reader agrees that under no circumstances is the author responsible for any losses, direct or indirect, that are incurred as a result of the use of the information contained within this document, including, but not limited to, errors, omissions, or inaccuracies.

Table of Contents

INTRODUCTION 1
   How to use the New Dad Playbook 3

CHAPTER 1: THE DAY YOU FIND OUT 5

CHAPTER 2: THE FIRST TRIMESTER 9
   Change Is Coming 11
   The Take Over 14
   When Exercise Is Not a Good Idea 15
   A Healthy Diet 17

CHAPTER 3: THE SECOND TRIMESTER 25
   How to Provide Relief 27
   20 Week Scan 28
   Birthing Classes/Antenatal Classes 30

CHAPTER 4: THE THIRD TRIMESTER 37
   How About That Baby? 40
   Packing for Three—The All Important Hospital Bag 41
   Plan Your Route 44

CHAPTER 5: PREPARATION 45
   Feeding, Sleeping, and Style 47
   Buying and Stocking the House 51

CHAPTER 6: THE DAY HAS COME 55
   No, Really, the Day Has Come 56
   According to a Change of Plans 59
   The Real Fun Starts 61

CHAPTER 7: THE FIRST THREE MONTHS 63
   Baby Development and Milestones 66
   Baby's Medical Needs 69
   Care For the Father 74

CHAPTER 8: 3–6 MONTHS 77
    WHAT TO DO TO HELP 79
    SLEEP TRAINING 82
    TEETHING AND FEEDING 85
    BABY PROOFING 90
    BUDGETING FOR NEW TIMES 95

CONCLUSION 99

REFERENCES 103

Introduction

You get home from work, pet the family dog, grab a beer, and sit down to watch the game. Maybe you're driving to the gym. Perhaps you waited many years, but hope has slipped away. Each scenario ends the same way. WE'RE PREGNANT!

Well, let's clear something up. YOUR PARTNER IS PREGNANT, which means you're going to be a father. You're in this together. No doubt about that, but some women are sensitive to the father saying 'we,' especially as the weight, back pain, and heat add on throughout the pregnancy. But, hey, congratulations to you and the life-changing blessing. You deserve to be excited and don't allow anyone to tell you otherwise.

The moment is overwhelming. Wrapping your mind around the things to come is an impossibility. Take it all in and wear a helmet because reality will hit you over the head sooner rather than later. Your emotions will switch between excitement, nervousness, worry, and fear. Relax. Every first-time dad experiences the same feelings. It's part of the role whether your entry into fatherhood was a masterful design or it took years of trying and prayers.

You have entered the season of fatherhood, which lasts for the rest of your life, so try to take it slow at first. Break down your journey to fatherhood into steps because the adventure is a lot to handle. The first step goes on for 39–40 weeks if time is on your side. The load on your shoulders is heavy as you dedicate yourself to caring for your partner and unborn child. The one thing that no one mentions is that life might seem lonely for the dad in the moments of pregnancy. As a male or non-binary person, you've likely never been pregnant before, so it's hard to understand what's going on inside your partner's belly. In fact, there might be a bit of jealousy forming because she gets to experience a unique bond as a result of carrying and then bringing life into this world. While she's turning into a queen, you're wrestling with who you are, who you want to be, and who you might become.

Can I be a better father than the one I had? That's a valid question. Too many men grew up suffering because they were without a good fatherly figure. It's hard to know what to do when you never had the guidance you deserved. It's the kind of thing that keeps you up at night when you know responsibility is at your door. Can we afford to raise children? Someone once said that if you're waiting until you can afford children to have them, then you'll wait forever. That's not to say that you and others aren't financially stable now. The thought behind it suggests that you never know what's going to come out of life. You might be set now, but do you know where your job is five years from now? The year 2020 taught the world that relying on your present is unreliable. Everything got flipped upside down, and "Can I afford life?" became a larger question than life itself. Parents have been making it work since the beginning of time. Guess what? Time hasn't run out yet, so be confident that you bringing a baby into this world is going to be okay. Will I break my baby? The last question seems out of leftfield but do trust that many men thought their strength was too much to hold a baby. You can rest assured that you aren't as physically imposing as you believe. Have your doubts, but know that the *New Dad Playbook to Win at Parenting* has the answers you're looking for.

The stress is natural. Your life is about to change, and that's not a bad thing. You are entering the happiest stage of your life, but it is not going to be easy. Remember, *you* also matter during this pregnancy. Who is taking care of you while you are attempting to micromanage the potentially chaotic pregnancy? Your family will suffer if you can't stay in the game both physically and mentally. Besides reading this book, what are you doing in life to help yourself? Don't say making money. What good is money if you aren't around to enjoy what it can provide for your family? You have to start relaxing and remembering that life is worth who you're spending it with.

Don't let life suffocate you before you have the chance to meet your son or daughter, or fingers crossed… a combination that makes up twins. Continue reading to gain a wealth of knowledge in preparation for becoming the best dad possible. The most important thing is you got this far, which means you understand that you're not ready. Keep going. You'll feel like you can instruct other first-time dads by the time you finish reading this book, but your hands will be full, so point them in this direction instead.

You have questions, and many answers are located in this book. Open your thinking box, and prepare yourself to confidently handle your partner's pregnancy, the birth of your child, and the first six months as a new family. Fatherhood awaits you, so let's get started.

How to use the New Dad Playbook

The following is a guide that will take you from conception to birth and walk you through the first six months of your child's life. You'll use the *New Dad Playbook to Win at Parenting* to find the answers to all of the questions you have about fatherhood, supporting your partner, and what it means for you as an individual. You're expected to adapt to this new world, but change isn't always easy. Use the information you'll acquire to learn what to do right before you have an opportunity to do it wrong. This book will help you make adjustments to your parenting approach and build your confidence as you progress to each stage. Remember, the *New Dad Playbook to Win at Parenting* isn't absolute. Raising each child is a unique adventure. Use the material in this book to discover the unique father in you.

Whether you're reading this book in advance for preparation or taking in the chapters as they apply to you, this book is meant to be referred back to time and time again. It's a written support system to provide you with the confidence necessary in preparation for you becoming the best dad to win at parenting.

Chapter 1:

The Day You Find Out

For many, a conversation about starting a family predates the commitment to the relationship. Parenting is a serious business, so knowing that your significant other is on the same page as you is essential before you start preparing for your little one. I'm sure you asked all the necessary questions about why she wants a baby with you. She probably didn't ask the same thing, but if she did, you must've answered correctly. Planning for a baby is full of excitement. What are you going to name the little prince or princess? Names are important for establishing legacy and identity. They have history. You wouldn't name your kid Brick (apologies if someone named Brick is reading this book). You might stock up on pregnancy tests from the local pharmacy. Your partner knows their cycle, so dates for blissful exploration could be marked on the calendar. Don't be surprised if she went ahead and added dates of her ovulation to your calendar as well. Part of the planning process is knowing what days are best suited for trying to conceive.

Ovulation is when the female body transports a mature egg into an ovary. Once it hits the fallopian tube, there's a window of 12–24 hours when the egg is ripe for fertilization, but you can still have sex other days and still have the possibility of the egg fertilizing. Your memories of health class probably bring forth thoughts of your swimmers traveling and surviving for up to five days while attempting to hit the spot which means that heating things up in the bedroom for five straight days before and on the day of ovulation can further improve your chances.

5

That's right, getting here was fun. If you're still in the planning stages, but you bought this book to start learning now, then go have some more fun in between turning the pages. Light those candles, get rid of those throw pillows, and turn on some music. The day will come when all the hard work pays off and you're hit with the blessing of pregnancy. It's worth the effort more than you'll ever realize. If your arrival to parenthood was unplanned, you are also in the right place—the unexpected and unprepared travel in the same boat.

I hope you stocked up on Body Armor, Gatorade, and coconut water. Hydration was and is key to providing you the energy to keep up the extracurricular bedroom activities. Some of you reading this understand how stressful it might have gotten if the nights of joyful planning took longer than expected. For those in the middle of the calculating conception… trust the process. Keep your lady stress-free and don't get into the habit of blaming yourself. You're in this together and that means staying calm and understanding that some things take time.

We have all heard the stories from other men about when or how they found out their partner was pregnant. Sometimes you receive a coded warning such as, "Babe, I'm late" or "My cousin had a dream about me swimming with fish." The dream thing sounds weird, doesn't it? There isn't any medical proof that certain dreams detect future arrivals, but many women and various cultures swear by them. The fish dream is more respected than any other animal dream when it comes to these old wives' tales. Although the prediction aspect tends to ring true, it's better to rely on modern methods of medical accuracy.

Your better half picks one of the many pregnancy tests you've been hoarding. She may or may not take the test in your presence. Finding out is a special moment, and emotions dictate how your domestic partner chooses to proceed. An action to squat away from you could be her way of shielding you from an undesirable outcome or she wants to keep a bit of unknown love to herself for a few minutes. The next five minutes might seem like an eternity, but don't take this as an opportunity to catch up on Madden or walk the dog. Wait for or with her. Your wife or partner stands in front of you holding a stick with a plus sign or two lines. She either tells you with words or her smile says it all. The test indicates that a baby is on the way. What do you do? The obvious answer is to double-check the test because you want to be sure. This is a big moment in your life. Everything can change. It's okay to get your hopes up. Chances are she probably took two different brands without you knowing, and the results are the same. You want her joy to be yours. Congratulate her, give her a hug, and say thank you. Now, give yourself a fist bump. Your swimmers are strong. What a relief.

What's the first thing you do now that it's confirmed she's pregnant? Do you tell the soon-to-be-grandparents? Should you call your best friends? The correct answer is to keep things between the two of you. It's hard, especially for the first child because your cup is spilling over with love, and telling the world is a must. Many first-time dads don't know this, but the beginning stages of pregnancy come with much anguish. The anticipation of confirmation is followed by the hopes of making it to the safe stage, which is usually the end of the first trimester. This period is between weeks 12 and 13, but your significant other is most likely at about four weeks when the test is taken.

Miscarriage is most common at the beginning of pregnancy. Research suggests that 80% of miscarriages occur within the first trimester (Marcin, 2018). If you're reading this handbook during the first trimester, understand that many factors cause miscarriages. The age of the expected mother plays a huge role. The likelihood of a miscarriage increases the older the person is, but age isn't all. Chromosomal abnormalities are responsible for half of all miscarriages. Neither of you can control what happens physically, but you can help alleviate the stress by coming together as a team. You're in this new world together.

So, if you guys haven't told anyone yet, don't. Agree to be a team of two for a little while longer. Look at the secret as a safety net instead of a lie. The information isn't to scare you, but it's to prepare you for the difficulties of becoming a parent. An unfortunate outcome is devastating, but dealing with a miscarriage in front of everyone before she's ready will break your hearts even more, so take your time with spreading the news. If the team decides to share before the 12-week mark, only tell the grandparents and your closest friends. Still, it's a good idea not to rush the announcement. The eight-week point might be when you want to start sharing to the select few. At that time, the doctors can detect a heartbeat. Your mothers will forgive you. Your fathers will understand. Her best friend might want to rip your head off, but she will come around. Besides, there's much more to handle during the first trimester, and you have to get ready.

Chapter 2:

The First Trimester

Understand that a decision to remain silent about the pending member to your family puts more pressure on both of you. You have to step up to the plate and take on more responsibilities. You are your partner's number one support system. The health and happiness of your girl help securely bring along the baby during the first stages of growth. You're probably wondering how the growing part is coming. In many instances, it's hard to see any physical changes early in the pregnancy. You know that your partner is expecting, but where is that baby bump you always see in the movies?

At four weeks, which is about the time you find out she's pregnant, the baby has a heartbeat. It looks like a little tadpole swimming around with organs while developing. At eight weeks, the embryo takes the form of a human with facial features, bone structure, developing limbs, and tooth buds. Believe it or not, with everything going on, the mother still can't feel the little one growing. By the end of the trimester, the now fetus is equipped with full limbs, fingernails and toenails, and the start of a voice box and external genitals. The changes are there, and they multiply at an alarming rate. One might think an invisible man or a ghost is pulling the strings of pregnancy symptoms, and they wouldn't be far off. The initial transformation escapes the naked eye, but the mother-to-be goes through a rush of physical, emotional, and mental attacks. Be ready to handle them with care and patience.

She'll want to track her symptoms, and you should do the same. It's time to stay in communication about what the future mother is experiencing with her body, as this is how you will best support her. Here's a pro tip: *all pregnancies are not created equal!* That's right, don't rely on all input from mothers of pregnancies past. Pay attention to the day-to-day feelings of your better half, and start doing so right away. Log every detail so the two of you can share it with the doctor. That's the OB/GYN (baby doctor) in the United States for those who don't know. While midwives do exist in the States, they're typically the main form of pregnant mom and baby care across the pond. Listen, some ailments don't align with the typical pregnancy starter list. The OB/GYN or midwife will notice when something is off, but it helps if he or she has the valuable details going into the first appointment. The number one priority for everyone involved is to produce the healthiest pregnancy possible. Here's another tip: don't be afraid to switch to another OB or midwife if your significant other is uncomfortable with the initial conversations at the appointments. No doctor is the same, and bedside manner isn't becoming of each medical professional. It's a long road from month one to month nine, and your family deserves the absolute best care.

So, we're logging the symptoms seven days a week. Pen to paper is fine, but make it easier on both of you by finding a decent pregnancy app. A good app helps keep you up-to-date with the baby's development as well as provides information about the mother's ever-changing body. Dads don't get the same baby connection the mothers receive during this time, but an app can bring you closer to your unborn child. You matter and it's okay to want a more loving bond with your child before you get to see them. These apps can be found on both the Apple App Store and the Google Play Store. There is so much out there that wasn't available to parents before. A good app goes a long way in helping you feel comfortable and informed during the pregnancy.

At your first prenatal appointment with your girl, make sure you have a list of all medications she's currently taking if this isn't her primary doctor's office. Lining up the different prescriptions at home and snapping a picture is a great idea because it saves time and you don't feel the pressure of having to pronounce some of those long medical names on the bottles. Having a photo of her prescriptions is also great if you need to take your partner to an emergency room during the pregnancy. The emergency room nurse is going to ask what your significant other is still taking. The information is already on file if your partner has been seen at that location since becoming pregnant, but the nurses will have to input everything into the system if not. The initial pregnancy appointment is met with a complete physical exam, tests for the unborn baby, and a look into the mother's medical history. Think about bringing information for your family medical history as well because it's good to know what pre-existing conditions plague your family, and the OB will want to make note of it as well. Testing will happen later in the pregnancy to check into possible anomalies, but having some information ahead of time is always great.

Change Is Coming

Do you remember those symptoms discussed earlier? They are not fun for the mother. Morning sickness is a real thing, but don't be fooled by the name. Bouts of nausea may trickle in throughout the day during the first trimester, and for a small selection, the spells decide to remain for the duration of the pregnancy. It's not a fun time no matter how much or little sickness the mother-to-be experiences. In some cases, queasy sensations and vomiting don't enter the equation; however, half of all pregnancies have reported the dreadful dance with the bucket and porcelain God. Your college days can probably relate to the dance of those expected mothers, but do yourself a favor and keep that quiet.

How do you get ready to help your spouse battle morning sickness? An attempt to rid the house of any nausea-inducing items won't do the trick because the cause for morning sickness has managed to evade the best medical authorities; however, the nausea phenomenon stems from somewhere and doctors have made educated guesses for the potential reasons. For one, the expecting parties are on a rollercoaster ride of constant chemical and physical alterations to their bodies. Imagine standing in the heat for two hours waiting in line for an amusement park ride, and you downed three beers and a bag of fried Oreos. Your stomach would most likely betray you. Now you can imagine what the pregnant host may feel every day for weeks on end. Motion sickness happens to be the cousin of morning sickness. It doesn't make sense, but a sensitivity to motion sickness keeps the pregnant body swaying uneasily.

It doesn't happen quite as often, but severe morning sickness strikes with a heavy hand when it rears its head. People often believe pregnancy nausea automatically equals constant vomiting, but that's not the case. Ejecting from the stomach more than three times per day is a telling sign that the sickness is approaching severe concerns. Be on the lookout for drastic weight loss or dehydration that leads to fewer bathroom breaks. You should expect your significant other to increase her bathroom use during the pregnancy. Call the OB/GYN or midwife if any of these concerns present themselves.

Other factors like exhaustion, unagreeable foods, and stress triggers may lead to normal morning sickness, but you don't need to overreact. Reassure your teammate that occasional vomiting, although unsettling, won't hurt her or the baby.

There are some measures to take that may help combat morning sickness to some degree. Mint is a great option to help settle the stomach. There are plenty of mint herbal teas to choose from at the grocery store. Chances are, your favorite coffee shop has a selection of mint-infused teas to purchase. The natural herb provides a calming sensation and relieves the pressures from headaches.

Citrus may also help bring some relief. Try getting the mom to drink water with fresh lemon by squeezing a bit of the juice into her cup or simply having her smell the citrus while taking a drink. Not only will the citrus fruit help with morning sickness, but adding it to water will increase its usefulness. Keeping hydrated reduces those queasy sensations on a normal day.

Fresh ginger is another option to help. Ginger is a proven natural remedy to handle queasiness. It's a strong root, so use it in moderation. Add it to tea or sip hot water that only has ginger steeping in the liquid. If your partner can't handle the strength of fresh ginger, you can opt for ginger snaps or ginger candies, but be careful with the sugar content of those options. Keeping a bag of ginger snaps or candies in both vehicles is a great idea for when motion sickness triggers her morning sickness. You can also keep crackers in the car to help with sickness. At home, a piece of toast or crackers will serve two purposes by settling the stomach and providing a snack opportunity.

Sipping on a hot cup of bone broth will warm the soul, provide health benefits, and decrease queasiness. It's a triple-play option any time of the year for a pregnant woman. You can also add things like lemon and ginger to the broth to provide a lighter taste and extra help to settle morning sickness.

These options are all healthy for your partner and easy to acquire.

The Take Over

Are you used to your partner getting up early and tackling the day? She goes to work, buys the groceries, cooks dinner, schedules appointments, washes and folds the laundry, and manages to do all of this with hours to spare in the day. That was a pre-pregnancy spouse. She was a real go-getter. It will pay dividends if you don't mention the person she used to be because expecting changes expectations. Fatigue has introduced itself and your best response is to allow your person to rest. Her hormones are running amok. Don't let these sometimes scary mood swings disarm you from doing what is right.

She can sleep in, take naps, and take it easy, but don't let your partner go into social media and streaming hibernation from life. Keep her moderately active. Exercise will increase blood flow and lower blood pressure, which decreases the risk of having a miscarriage. Your significant other will feel more energized and she won't suffer from gaining too much unhealthy baby weight. The benefits of working out don't end there. Increased exercise during pregnancy results in a higher success rate for a vaginal delivery. Most women prefer a natural delivery over a cesarean (C-section), and the recovery time is heightened by routine workouts during the nine months. If daily workouts were part of the regularly scheduled program pre-pregnancy, then continue as planned if the doctor gives the thumbs up; however, have the future mother ease into a workout plan if exercise is a new thing. Swimming, walking, aerobics, stationary biking, and light yoga are great options to increase healthy activity for at least a few hours per week. Using a stationary bike can work wonders. Put it up in the living room or bedroom, or wherever there's a TV, so your partner can get on the bike while her favorite show is on. You also have to start finding more time to get or stay fit, so you may want to purchase another bike if necessary. Show her how committed you are to taking this ride (no pun intended) together. Working out as a couple is motivating, attractive, and strengthens that bond. Check with your local gym to see what yoga classes are available. If cost is a problem, you can find yoga instructors on YouTube. Buy a few yoga mats and blocks and support her at home. Do your best downward dog and help with those stretches. Sign her up for pregnancy swimming classes at a local pool or YMCA. Time in the pool is relaxing, but water exercises are highly beneficial for your partner's health. It's heart-healthy and decreases high blood pressure. Keeping high blood pressure in check is one of the number one priorities for pregnant women. If it skyrockets, the chances of an extreme early or emergency delivery increase. Avoid high-impact workouts that shake her about or potentially cause harm to the stomach. Pregnancy isn't the time to take that ski vacation or horseback riding lessons.

When Exercise Is Not a Good Idea

There are reasons for some women to avoid what may be considered helpful exercises during pregnancy. Some physical activity could increase certain problems that exist during the nine months. We mentioned that swimming is great for providing a heart-healthy pregnancy, but not all hearts can handle the pool and other physical activities. If your wife or partner already has a heart condition that restricts blood flow, then exercise should be reconsidered. The body relies on the heart to pump blood. The circulation system is responsible for moving blood, nutrients, and oxygen throughout the body. A weak heart with poor blood flow will restrict the blood from moving to the umbilical cord.

Preeclampsia is another concern that restricts the use of exercise. Preeclampsia forms around the 20th week of pregnancy. The condition causes blood pressure to skyrocket, and if it doesn't get under control, the mother and baby are at risk. Quite often, emergency deliveries take place, and they happen earlier than one would ever like. The medical team would have to pump a steroid into the mother that helps develop the lungs of the baby to give them a fighting chance when arriving so early. These emergency deliveries can take place sometimes eight weeks, nine weeks, or more before the expected delivery date. Severe preeclampsia is closely monitored, and bed rest for the remainder of the pregnancy is often considered in an effort to get the mother-to-be closer to the actual delivery date.

Bleeding in the vaginal area becomes a serious concern when it occurs within the second and third trimesters. Workouts will not do anything but increase the bleeding. It's important to know that vaginal bleeding will not stop from four months on. Once it arrives, it isn't going to leave. Falling under the category of preterm labor delivers another "no exercise" clause in the pregnancy contract. Preterm labor may occur from 2o weeks and up to week 37 of the pregnancy. A premature birth makes it harder for the baby. Like with preeclampsia, the baby comes out fighting for their life. Time in the NICU will likely be necessary. Pregnant mothers who are expecting twins or more already get designated with the preterm label.

It's not to say that pregnant women who fall into the "no exercise" zone can't have a healthy pregnancy, it's that strenuous activity and stress make it harder to have a healthy pregnancy. It's scary to think that your child might have an increased chance of entering this world with a decreased chance of surviving.

A Healthy Diet

You might already be a modern man who takes on his fair share of family responsibility. Great, now take on more. Encourage healthy eating from the start by doing all of the grocery shopping. Healthy eating is essential for the average person, but it has to amp up for pregnant women. An expecting mother's body deals with a high volume of demands. Meeting those starts with an ideal diet to provide healthy fetus growth. Take the time to learn the dos and don'ts of pregnancy eating. Balance is the key. You might be surprised to learn that close to 90% of people in the United States fail to consume the suggested 2.5 cups of vegetables per day (Newman, 2021). You don't need the math to figure out that you and your partner probably fall in line with those numbers, but if you are getting your 2.5 cups, then great; however, it may still be time to ramp this up since your partner is now eating for two! It's always ideal to fill those plates with more vegetables than protein. Keep it as simple as possible too. Don't add that cheese to your broccoli, cauliflower, and salads. Properly cook your vegetables if you don't want the raw option. Overcooking pulls out too many nutrients. Familiarize yourself with microgreens. You'll find that they often contain more vitamins and minerals than their larger counterparts. So, hit your local farmers markets or higher ranking stores to buy the freshest vegetables and fruits. She should have close to two cups of fruits per day. 100% juice is okay in moderation because consuming too much increases the sugar intake.

A variety of foods from these groups is a great choice because who wants to eat a spinach chicken salad five days per week. Be careful with the selections because some options are healthier than others. Rice sounds like a winner compared to mashed potatoes, and pasta with fresh marinara minus the meatballs seems safe. DON'T ASSUME. Instead, take the time to learn about complex carbohydrates because they will help reduce exhaustion and add necessary fiber to the pregnant belly. Such foods include healthy starchy vegetables like butternut squash, farro, and sweet potatoes. Listen, you can do wonders with these selections and impress your partner at the same time. Who knew your knowledge of cuisine could move beyond steak, pastries, and fast food? Instagram, Pinterest, YouTube, Facebook, and other platforms knew. Utilize those sites to learn new recipes to keep you and your better half eating properly. That's right, your health is equally important. There are amazing chefs online ready to provide the food guidelines for creating healthier menus.

- Maddie Lymburner: 312k Instagram followers. She's a fitness expert who promotes healthy living, healthy cooking, and healthy fitness.

- Agatha Achindu: 15k and counting Instagram followers. Agatha is a nutritionist specialist. Her healthy cooking oils and tips are benefiting chefs on a global scale.

- The Buddhist Chef: 300k Instagram followers. The Buddhist Chef helps you find peace and tranquility with the foods you cook in the kitchen.

These chefs' presence on social media can provide you with the confidence of making the right decision when choosing what recipes to prepare for your family.

There are plenty of chefs and home cooks online who care about the well-being of pregnant mothers everywhere. Search to find what foods are the best. Cravings might have your partner asking for a juicy burger, pizza, or boxes of Girl Scout cookies. While it's okay for your partner to divulge in these treats occasionally, you have the capability of curving an unhealthy appetite. Good protein choices include fish, chicken, eggs, legumes, nut butter, lean beef, and tofu.

You're taking on more responsibility than you figured. Do you have the time to commit to proper food prep? Think about getting a small deep freezer for your kitchen or garage. It will come in handy during this time. You can meal prep to make your transition into the kitchen much easier. Meal prepping does more than take away stress in the kitchen. Adding this plan to your life will save you time. You can come home from a long day at work and not worry about staging everything in the kitchen before cooking. You can pull a couple of prepped meals from your new freezer, heat, and serve. You can also ask your partner if she wouldn't mind taking a few of the fresh-like freezer meals out earlier in the day to say even more time. You can have a month's worth of meals ready to go and only spend one day prepping all of them for the freezer.

Time still isn't your friend when it comes to working the kitchen duties. That's okay. If your partner is still working, the two of you can find a food service that prepares meals for you. You would be surprised at how cost-efficient some of the places are. You can go online, select what type of food you're looking for, and how many meals. In many ways, you will get fresher ingredients and better-tasting items at a good cost. Plus, you can choose to go in a healthier direction to benefit the mother-to-be. Don't be afraid to utilize the resources to find the right company. Great food at an amazing price is only a search engine away. Here are some options to learn more about.

- HelloFresh
- CookUnity
- My Home Chef
- DineInDulge

When going with a quality food delivery service, keep in mind that many offer first-time discounts. Many companies provide a 50% off option for the first full week of deliveries. The hope is that you'll enjoy the professional high-end ingredients so much that you won't mind paying full price to come back. We spend so much money buying foods with increased preservatives or on items that we don't get around to cooking before they go bad, we don't even need to discuss how much money we throw away at restaurants. You can also earn a discount from the chef options for referrals. With the information provided, it's great to seriously think about going this route. Whatever you can do to save money and time will only make the pregnancy go by in a much more enjoyable and chilled manner.

Another resource to explore is the network of family and friends who will be over the moon when they discover that your team is having a baby. You would be surprised at how many people are willing to help when that kind of great news happens. Don't lay everything out there and explain that you're struggling to figure things out. Nicely ask who would be willing to cook some meals for a few months to help out the mother-to-be. Your best option is to come up with a plan. Type out a list of ingredients that you guys like, don't like, and can't consume (because of pregnancy and allergies). Next, feel free to add some recipe ideas that your partner is partial to making or enjoying. People who help won't mind a list that caters to the mother-to-be. This next part is the most important of them all—make sure they understand that you aren't asking them to pay for anything. You're asking for help with the labor aspect, but the money is coming from your wallet. You simply don't have the time to constantly cook, and you don't want your significant other and unborn child suffering from a lack of nutrients because ordering pizza is convenient. To sweeten the pot, you can offer up your kitchen for them to prepare everything. That will keep them from dirtying up their kitchens. They might clean up the mess for you, but you should be okay taking that charge if necessary.

So, you're getting an idea of how the diet needs to change. Now, go buy some extra water bottles. The bigger, the better. Most people should increase their water intake, but pregnant women must do it even more. Hydration is vital for the mother and fetus, and drinking more water will naturally decrease hunger. Be careful with some of those hydrating drink options. Gatorade and Body Armor are great for replenishing the body with electrolytes after a good workout, but what type of workouts is your partner doing? If there isn't a lot of calories being burned, then that type of replenishing isn't the greatest of choices. Those drinks contain extra sugars that aren't ideal for your pregnant partner. It's a bad idea for a person to consume those beverages as a casual drink anytime, so it's a hard no during pregnancy. If she does want something different to wet the pallet other than water, juice, or tea... get the Gatorade Zeros and Body Armor Lytes since they don't contain added sugar.

Everything is coming at you fast, but you have never been in a more important role. Here's what not to do. Avoid serving meats that are between rare and medium in temperature. Of course, any civilized human knows that the best tasting cuts of steak contain flavorful pink juices, but those aren't what's best for your unborn child. Certain foods cause food poisoning and other illnesses during pregnancy. Cook those meats, and to be safe, perhaps you should only do well-done temps. Since we're on the subject of bad pregnancy foods, say goodbye to your regularly scheduled sushi (sashimi) dates, other uncooked shellfish, and fish with mercury. Oysters, scallops, and clams fit into the category. Those oyster bars and lightly smoked scallops have to wait. Thoughts have changed over the years on whether or not sushi is a no-no during pregnancy, but think about the risk versus reward aspect. Here is a list of high mercury fish to stay clear of.

- Shark
- Orange roughy
- Swordfish
- Southern bluefin tuna
- Barramundi

The dos and don'ts of what to eat and avoid are constantly changing. It's best to ask your medical professional for advice on what to do. Take the time to make the best decision for you and your partner. Here's a link that might help. Go to https://www.healthline.com/nutrition/11-foods-to-avoid-during-pregnancy#Food-Fix:-What-to-Eat-When-Pregnant

Protein is part of the program that is a necessity for your partner during pregnancy. Your unborn baby counts on protein for healthy development and growth. Your spouse or girlfriend has to increase their protein intake if she normally consumes less than her body requires; however, don't allow her cravings or your cooking to go overboard. Too much protein will block your child's fetal tissue development inside the womb. The right amount of protein allows the body to create more blood to support the changes within. The importance of extra blood rises during the second and third trimesters.

Some people like to lean toward a high-protein, low-carb diet or meal plan. Pregnancy only requires an extra 300 calories per day, which doesn't sound like a lot when you see that number. Sticking to a high-protein, low-carb diet would lead you toward adding more protein; however, adding meat produces more calories than the 300 extra she should consume. The risk results in unhealthy weight gain. Try getting those extra calories from more vegetables on the plate. Besides, adding vegetables allows for larger servings and more energy. Get those calories up for her, but do it in the right way.

Instead of focusing on the calories, you should pay attention to the grams of protein the mother-to-be is receiving. Forty-five grams of protein per day was the requirement before she got pregnant (Ipatenco, 2017). The increase due to pregnancy only increases to 70 grams of protein per day (Ipatenco, 2017). You can easily get those numbers by increasing fish (anchovies are a great option), nuts, cheese, beans, and lentils intake. Meat doesn't have to always be the go-to for eating protein.

The last order of business for taking over the grocery buying and preparing the menu has to do with beverages outside of water and juice. Sure, some physicians say a few glasses of red wine per week won't directly cause harm to the fetus, but encourage your partner to abstain from drinking alcohol from day one. She'll develop a healthy habit during the first trimester that will benefit everyone for the full pregnancy. There actually isn't a known safe amount of alcohol one can digest while carrying; however, it's proven that the umbilical cord passes the alcohol in the blood to the unborn child. Caffeine is the other ingredient in drinks (and some snacks) that you want to cross off of the list. Some sodas, energy drinks, teas, and everyone's favorite, coffee, are gone for the next nine months. Caffeine increases the risk of miscarriages, so stay clear of energy jolting drinks. Rumor has it that decaffeinated coffee has the same great taste as regular. Don't listen to rumors. Oh, this next point is key to any first-time dad. You obviously can drink alcohol and coffee during this time, but your first go-around at this should include sacrifice. A good rule of thumb for dads is no coffee during the first successful pregnancy, coffee away from the mother during a second pregnancy, and a "screw it" attitude for three or more.

For more information on what drinks to avoid during pregnancy, you should once again reach out to the OB or midwife. Further information can be found if you go to https://www.whattoexpect.com/pregnancy/eating-well/what-to-drink-during-pregnancy.aspx

Chapter 3:

The Second Trimester

The first trimester has come and gone. Like most pregnancies, those 12 weeks were full of lessons. You were starting to settle in and figure a few things out. You have managed to relieve some stress by taking on the chores and trying new recipes. Compared to your partner's expertise, you're falling short, but as a soon-to-be dad, things are looking great. Information overload has occurred due to the many females in your life telling you what and what not to do. The advice is taken with a grain of salt. The mother-to-be appreciates your role even if she doesn't mention it out loud.

The baby continues to grow at a rapid rate, but the difference is, you start to notice. Your partner's belly is getting bigger. It's a significant moment for all dads. Before, it was hard to wrap your mind around the phenomenal changes happening daily. Now, your eyes can see what your heart was trying to feel. It's okay to pause and smile. Appreciate your part in writing the beautiful story that you and your partner are witnessing. Do you want some more good news? Morning sickness usually creeps away by week 13, which is a relief for the mother. The second trimester is like bringing balance to the force. In this case, her hormones are the things that have found balance. Nausea is gone and now you know for sure the unsettling stomach was caused by the baby and not your cooking. Also, those first-trimester mood swings have gone into hiding, making way for a happy camper with much more energy. Cool, right? But the changes don't stop there.

Your significant other has traded in the vomiting for body pain. Yes, discomfort continues, but in a much different way. Her muscles and joints will be screaming for relief, and you will want to offer your help. Make sure you check with the OB or midwife to see what is safe for the mother and unborn child. Both professionals will most likely approve the usage of acetaminophen, commonly known as Tylenol, to deal with pain. Make sure you check whatever bottle you're grabbing. You don't want to give your partner Aleve, Motrin, Advil, or any other medications that contain aspirin or ibuprofen because they may cause birth defects. Quite often, there are items that the doctors told you all to avoid during the first trimester that are now safe to use during the second, so ask about those as well.

As the baby grows, the mother's bones move to make room for the new edition and to prepare the body for the baby's eventual move through the birth canal. Carrying the weight adds stress to the back, while the moving bones add aches to the hip and pelvis area. Slow blood circulation also occurs because the mother-to-be retains more fluid to accommodate her roommate. Signs of her body experiencing discomfort from retained fluid include swelling of the ankles, face, and hands. Leg pain is also common during the second trimester as the baby strains the nerves and blood vessels that travel to the mother's legs. You can expect to hear complaints about leg pain throughout the night. Sleeping on her back will increase cramping in the legs, which could lead to deep vein thrombosis (DVT). Watch for swelling in one of her legs, which is a sign of DVT and a cause for alarm. The condition forms blood clots in the leg, and if it goes untreated, it may result in a pulmonary embolism.

Another change that often takes place during this time is an increased libido for women. Estrogen and progesterone levels spike to support the growth inside the mother's belly. At the same time, HCG levels reduce. For the mother, this is one of the reasons nausea has been replaced with higher energy levels. Blood flow to the vulva and vaginal lubrication rise, resulting in an increased sex drive.

How to Provide Relief

You don't like seeing your significant other in pain. Knowledge and a move to action are your best options to help her during this time. Purchase a body pillow that will help your partner adjust to sleeping on her side as opposed to her back. Not only will this ease the tension in her back, but it will help improve circulation in her legs to prevent DVT. Back pain and poor circulation aren't the only things that make sleeping more difficult during the second trimester. Those tricky hormones decide to restrict breathing by blocking the nose. It might not be a cold or sinus infection, but a stuffy nose is unbearable at any time. The good news is that you can make a quick trip to the store to purchase a saline nasal spray. It's perfectly safe for the mother and unborn child. You should provide a quick massage to her calf muscles before she goes to sleep. Cramps are known to happen in the legs while sleeping throughout the second trimester, and a tight leg cramp is enough pain to wake up anyone from a good sleep.

If things went well during the first trimester, then routine exercise remains part of the program. Healthy physical activity supports the back and leg muscles making her body more flexible as the baby continues to grow. Ask your OB or midwife if alternative methods are suitable for your spouse to support relaxation during pregnancy. Acupuncture and massage therapy are safe approaches to providing relief from pregnancy pain if the medical professionals sign off first.

Acupuncture is also an excellent resource to fight against headaches if Tylenol is unwanted or doesn't provide help. Some parents-to-be rather not use medicine at all, so look into more of those natural and alternative solutions. Diet continues to be a proven factor in addressing all types of physical and mental problems. Make sure your partner continues to hydrate, and don't let her skip meals. Don't forget about you either. Your focus on her can't be so great that you start forgetting to eat and drink regularly. A good tip to help her manage headaches is to keep a food log. Note what she eats and what time a headache starts. There could be a correlation between certain foods and headaches.

What about her increased sex drive? You might have dealt with your partner not wanting to explore between the sheets during the first trimester due to the morning sickness; however, her hormones are turning things around throughout the second trimester. Take the time to have a conversation to see what the two of you want. If sex is on the table, discuss how you want to proceed to adjust to her changing body. Communication is a form of intimacy and talking things out provides comfort for both parties. Besides, if sex wasn't in the cards for the first leg of pregnancy, you might be feeling frustrated. Talking about and discovering different positions could bring enjoyment for the two of you, and it's safe for the baby. Pregnancy doesn't always mean no sex for the foreseeable future.

20 Week Scan

The Second Trimester Fetal Development Anomaly Scan happens at the 2o week mark, and it's the most essential prenatal screening test. It screens for abnormalities and offers diagnosis from a specialist. So what exactly does the scan achieve? On the comforting side, it is able to show your child's body in full display. You'll see the arms, legs, fingers, toes, and prominent facial features. You might not understand what you're viewing, but the specialist will walk you through everything. They will determine the functionality of your baby's anatomy and identify the internal organs. We live in a time where most pregnancies are healthy, so this scan is there to bring peace to the parents to show that what they imagined is coming true.

Should something abnormal be detected, parents and doctors will have the time to decide the best course of action. Treatment for the unborn child can be implemented throughout the pregnancy, and certain discoveries can wait until after delivery to start working on healing.

The anomaly scan will determine if your baby has defects like clubfeet, heart problems, spinal damage, and even down syndrome. No parent wants to hear that their child is dealing with any type of health concern. Fathers go into protection mode as soon as they find out a baby is on the way. You will naturally feel helpless during the scan, and that feeling might increase if the results are undesirable. You're not alone. It's a great time to realize that you can't take on everything. Sometimes your role is to listen and understand the best way to handle the scary moments. Know that any possible defect is not the fault of you or your partner. Come together and be ready to love your child with your whole heart.

The anomaly scan will take approximately 30 minutes to run. You can trust the person running the scan; it will either be a doctor who specializes in prenatal diagnosis or a prenatal sonographer specialist. You and your partner will have access to a screen that displays 3D images of your baby in real-time. The doctor will analyze everything and compare the anomaly scan to all other scans and information from the pregnancy.

Ask any questions to gain the answers that will make sure you and your partner are comfortable when leaving the office.

Birthing Classes/Antenatal Classes

Have you discussed attending pregnancy classes with your spouse or girlfriend? By now, you've soaked up pregnancy knowledge throughout this handbook. You're bookmarking the best notes and even sharing details with your partner. The ultimate goal is to make sure that you, as a new dad, will win at every stage. Information is wonderful, but navigating birth is tricky, messy, and unpredictable for soon-to-be mothers and fathers. That's why taking a class is beneficial. You learn what you don't know, and it's a chance to experience the wonders of pregnancy with other couples. Bonding with those in the same boat as you builds community and understanding.

Birthing classes are common in the United States whereas antenatal classes are typical outside of the states. You can't go wrong with either type because in short, they are courses that help the parents prepare for labor, delivery, and what comes after. In most cases, antenatal classes are run by a midwife or similar, or you can go the private route and take one that's run by a doula. There are several ways to approach these preparation classes. Some couples opt for an all-day lesson due to scheduling conflicts. That's okay, you'll be able to soak up as much information as possible, and you will leave feeling more ready for the big day than you previously felt. If time allows the two of you to take a more steady approach, many instructors do weekly classes that cover new information along the way. Are you worried about the cost of signing up for a parenting course? Don't be. Insurance covers the cost of many birthing and antenatal classes. If insurance doesn't work out, there are free parenting courses available in several areas. Virtual is another way to go, especially since the pandemic of 2020. The online option provides safety and security for anyone wondering how to handle pregnancy in the Covid and post-covid era.

So, taking these classes are sounding more and more logical. Call your doctor, midwife, or your doula to have the discussion with them as well. Secure a letter of medical necessity from them that spells out the need for the pregnant host to take parenting classes. Insurance companies often require the letter for approval. Great, now you need to go through the steps of double-checking your insurance before picking a facility. If you have dealt with insurance companies before, you know that they may require more than your basic identity qualifications to get things started. Be ready to recite your diagnosis code and your current procedural terminology code (CPT code). The code is S9436 for CPT and Z32.2 for diagnosis education courses. Once you make the call and give the proper information, the insurance company can talk you through the next steps to take.

Check to see if you can use your health savings account (HSA) or flexible spending account (FSA) before scheduling an appointment for parenting classes. If you don't know, these types of accounts are pre-taxed and can be used to help with medical expenses. FSA represents a line of credit. HSA requires the person to have a high deductible health plan, but both FSA and HSA allow you to cover medical bills and copays, which is why you want to utilize one during pregnancy time if you and your partner have it. You or your partner might have one of these options included in your employee benefits packages. People don't always do a deep dive into what their packages include, so go ahead and pull yours out to take a look. When it comes to an FSA, you lose what you don't use.

You have the approval of the doctor or midwife to take parenting classes for the needs of the unborn child. Your insurance company has notified you that birthing or antenatal courses are covered by your policy. Don't start attending the ones that cost without getting an itemized receipt. In most cases, insurance coverage isn't provided without that proof of purchase. If doing an itemized receipt is unfamiliar territory, then follow along below and make a note. You need the exact cost of the training, whether it's a one-time fee or charged per week. Your significant other must be named as the patient. If you're not married and the program falls under your insurance, then make sure you check to see if they will cover her. The dates you participated have to be logged and specify what type of service was provided. Different courses handle various training techniques, and some offer more than others. Lastly, list the educator's name or the name of the provider along with the location. Providing those details will save you from getting stuck with the fees. In some instances, the place providing the service will give you or the mother a certification of completion that you can send in as verification.

Birthing or antenatal classes will bring balance to your time in the delivery room. These classes will run through most or all of the steps. You will understand how to coach your partner through breathing, contractions, and making that last push before seeing why it's all worth it. Your instructor knows what they are doing, and they will make sure you both walk away feeling confident.

Their job is to teach you techniques and reduce anxiety when the actual moment gets too real. You and your partner will learn how to breathe properly, relax, and learn how to distract from the labor pain and possible hours of waiting. If breathing could take away all of the pain, there wouldn't be a need to take these classes. The course will demonstrate several labor positions to get into that will help fight through the back pain. Your job will be to remember these positions to help your partner transition into them while in labor. Different labor positions also help the baby line up with the pelvis. You'll find that getting the baby to line up properly can potentially speed up labor. Who wouldn't want that process to go faster?

Next is to decide what type of birthing classes you and your partner wish to take. We mentioned before that not every training course is the same. Some only provide you and the mother with pain management strategies, breastfeeding techniques, and how to have a delivery free of medicine. There has never been a reason for you to know about these things, so read ahead to get an idea of what option to discuss at home.

HypnoBirthing, also known as The Mongan Method, has been around since 1989. This technique puts a focus on the preparation that helps deliver a peaceful and beautiful birth for the women. That's not all, this specialized method also puts a focus on the man involved. HypnoBirthing educators find the psychological and physical well-being to be equal in all parties of the pregnancy, which is the host, the father, and the baby. The proven method is meant to take place wherever you and your girl decide to have the baby. It has been said that the feeling evokes a meditation vibe. HypnoBirthing uses special breathing techniques, a focus on positive body toning, relaxation, visualization, meditative practices, and an understanding of nutrition. The idea is to dispel the scary birthing myths and bridge the gap between the mother, the body, and delivery to normalize all aspects of birthing. Should you decide to go with HypnoBirthing, you will find this practice stateside, online, and internationally.

You have probably heard of Lamaze at one time or another and understand that the name is associated with pregnancy. The Lamaze Method is one of the oldest techniques used during delivery and puts forth an effort to make the process more natural. Lamaze breathing techniques are what people hear about the most. They help reduce labor pain for the mother. Although breathing strategies were the main focus early on, Lamaze International has prided itself in expanding its knowledge to become more relevant over the years. The original practice was at risk of dropping off as more modern teachings were developed to fully serve the mother and child. Lamaze added a focus on massage therapy, movement, and hydrotherapy, and they started addressing options for utilizing medicine for pain and medical interventions, which wasn't something they did in their early decades of operation. Natural childbirth remains the goal, but Lamaze instructors aim to educate the parents to ensure they are truly informed before giving medical consent. You can expect the Lamaze course to not be overcrowded because they keep the limit to 12 couples. The total meeting time is around 12 hours. Couples are encouraged to start attending classes at the seventh-month mark.

A more holistic strategy makes use of a plan called Birthing from Within. Pam England, a certified nurse, midwife, and natural birth advocate, developed the method as a way to implement her ideas that the power of birth is a natural rite of passage. The course follows key points about natural deliveries as it pertains to trusting the body the same as hypnotherapy and others, but Birthing from Within is more about teaching the host about the "mindset of resilience" rather than simply equipping couples with a list of 'tools.' This is more about making pregnancy and birth a journey of self-discovery, and the arts and philosophy play a significant role. Educators will show you and your partner how to use journaling, poetry, and visualization as they lead you through an art session that helps awaken the mind. The courses will also mix in a "labor theater" group sharing to provide beneficial explorations of belief among the participants. Online courses are an option as well.

The last option we will explore is The Bradley Method, which teaches couples how to usher in a baby together. This class also wants to encourage the use of a doula for the time of delivery. It's another viable choice if you and your significant other want a medicine-free birth. Before The Bradley Method, men weren't considered a need in the delivery room. This plan's idea for father inclusion is also known as "husband-coached natural childbirth." The 12-week course (starting during the fifth month of pregnancy) teaches the importance of a nutrient-rich diet, exercise, and an understanding of all aspects of pregnancy, including postpartum care. You are the coach, and it's your job to utilize relaxation techniques and serve as the mother-to-be's advocate during labor and delivery. Advocating will fit you because the course guides you through understanding when medical interventions are necessary, how to avoid birthing complications, and coping with drastic changes to the birth plan. Your inclusion in this training will strengthen the connection you have with your partner for the remainder of the pregnancy and beyond. Something to note is that The Bradley Method takes a stronger stance than most against medicine involvement during pregnancy and childbirth. Understand that some issues can't avoid medical interventions, or that it's extremely dangerous should you stick to your guns. The Bradley Method may give you and the mother-to-be false hope.

However the two of you decide what class is best is up to your level of comfort, interest, and beliefs. All classes, including those not listed in this handbook, have the same goal in mind. Doctors, midwives, instructors, and trainers only want what's best for the mother, baby, and even you. Don't forget to check with the insurance companies and your employer to see how much coverage is available to you and your partner. Talk to the delivery team at the hospital or medical center where the birth will take place. See if that facility includes parenting, birthing, or antenatal classes in the package. If pricing is an issue, contact the free clinics and family resources in your area to see what they have available. Lastly, please don't let a lack of availability in your town stop you and your partner from childbirth education. The internet is your friend throughout the process. Happy class hunting.

Chapter 4:

The Third Trimester

Your partner has carried your seed for 26 weeks. Breathe a little bit because you don't have too much longer to go. Your lady may have suddenly found a good amount of energy at this point in the pregnancy, and she might start taking to cleaning for the first time since you took over the cleaning responsibilities. The urge to organize and clean at this stage is known as nesting. Nesting occurs when the soon-to-be mother throws herself into a frenzy to get the house ready for the baby's arrival. The closer she gets to the delivery date, the more nesting she might try to accomplish. Many believe that nesting indicates that labor has started, but those rumors don't hold much weight. The time of year could show why your pregnant partner decided to resume housekeeping duties. Springtime naturally gets people into the business of making things shine around the house. The holidays are the same because people want to tidy up for decorations and traveling relatives.

Are you worried about your spouse or girlfriend doing too much at this time? It's understandable. After all, you implemented a game plan and you wouldn't want anything to ruin it this far into the pregnancy; however, you can sit back and relax. As long as she isn't attempting to lift heavy objects, your partner and unborn child are safe. Just make sure she doesn't take to using bleach and other strong chemicals to clean.

Outside of nesting, your job continues to be to watch out for alarming signs and to take care of your partner. The finish line is near, but her body is still constantly changing because the baby isn't finished growing, which strains your partner's muscles and ligaments. By now, sleep might be a distant cousin. The back pain has increased tremendously, which makes it difficult for your significant other to get proper rest at night. Also, the baby is pushing on the bladder, which results in more trips to the bathroom due to the added pressure. Another cause of sleepless nights is breathing, or should I say a lack of breathing? The baby is cramming the abdominal area, causing tension when the mother tries to inhale deeply. Think about how you feel taking a deep breath when your ribs are compromised.

Other changes happen within. Apologies are given if you grew accustomed to your partner's increased sex drive during the second trimester. More than likely, she isn't interested in the third trimester. Hormones and a lack of comfort decrease the females' libido as the due date approaches. There are other ways you can connect with her. Lay in bed and rub her back or feet. Talk about what you miss and look forward to doing when she's ready to explore that physical connection again. These are moments where the two of you can build a stronger emotional connection, which will benefit you equally; however, you will notice an increase in heat another way. The unborn child radiates body heat, which causes the mother's skin temperature to rise. She will feel the results. A summer pregnancy will only intensify sensations of heat.

On the outside, you will continue to notice swelling in her ankles, feet, hands, face, and arms from the retained fluid. Tell her it's only the edema and it will go away. As an added bonus, your use of medical terms might impress her. Another possible change is hair growth, which she can blame hormones for yet again. Increased hormone stimulation of hair follicles generates growth on the legs, arms, and face at times. These are the results of the baby growing inside, so don't make your lady feel self-conscious about any extra hair. Remember, the fetus is pulling and stretching those muscles, so you'll see those results on your partner's skin in the form of stretch marks. They will be more noticeable on her stomach, but they may also occur on her breast, butt, and thighs as well. One thing you can count on is that the third trimester will be the most uncomfortable one. There are products, such as bio-oil, that many dermatologists recommend to prevent stretch marks and take care of existing scars. The oil (in name only) leaves the skin feeling fresh and hydrated while doing its best to ease your partner's self-consciousness. You should go to trusted sites to read reviews on the product and ask the OB or midwife for their opinion before purchasing any wellness item to use during pregnancy. It's a good idea to keep your excitement about pregnancy beautifiers to yourself if your partner hasn't expressed any concerns. There's no need to increase her self-consciousness if the thought was never there.

How can you continue to ease your significant other's mental anguish and physical pain? For starters, check on her throughout the night. You don't have to set alarms or anything, but there are some measures you can take. Help her to bed and then stay up a little longer. Tell her you want to do some extra cleaning or catch a game while she goes to sleep, but that you'll join her soon. She needs to sleep on her side from 28 weeks and up until the baby arrives. Sleeping on her back reduces the baby's oxygen supply by restricting the blood flow to the womb, which may increase the chance of a stillbirth. Plenty of people switch from their side to their back in the middle of the night. If that happens to your partner, you can gently roll her to the side when you go to bed. You can also use that body pillow you previously bought to help her make that side sleeping adjustment and prop some extra pillows behind her back.

How About That Baby?

Well, the baby is becoming quite impressive in that uterus. You can't see the changes, but the little guy or gal is growing and developing very nicely during the third trimester. Expect the fetus to transition to a head-down position. He or she naturally knows to make that turn in preparation for delivery. Isn't science amazing? Each week of the third trimester comes with something uniquely different about you and your partner's baby.

The baby is nearing 10 inches in length and should weigh just over a few pounds by week 28 of the pregnancy. The eyelashes have developed, and your child can partly open the eyelids for preparation to see the world. Can you picture them blinking? The central nervous system is functioning with the ability to manage body temperature and direct rhythmic breathing movements. Have you thought about pinching those chubby cheeks in the future? Well, the baby is working on storing fat in the 29th week. White fat deposits begin to form under the skin, which is a crucial part of your child's healthy arrival. Ideally, infants are born with at least 15% body fat to use for brain development, fighting against sickness, and use for energy. How do you think newborns have the vigor to constantly cry? Those fat composites also help with kicking, grasping, and stretching in the womb.

Let's get into the rest of the third-trimester milestones.

Your baby is nearing three pounds, which is the weight of a bike helmet. The lungs are preparing for breathing air outside of the mother, but in the meantime, the baby starts breathing and swallowing fluids in the womb.

Life in the mother's belly is no longer the comfort it once was. Space shrinks as the fetus is now gaining half a pound each week. Your child has learned to fold itself into the fetal position to accommodate for the lack of legroom. He or she is rotating the head side to side to build up the neck muscles for the anticipated journey. All five senses are already being used. Now the fetus has grown to the size of a medium teddy bear but with a bit more weight as they inch closer to four pounds.

Time is running out as the baby increases all functions at a rapid rate. He or she is going through a lot, and they need to rest. Expect the child to enter deep sleep inside the womb part of the time, and rapid eye movement (REM) the rest. Yes, your unborn child is dreaming. Perhaps they have gotten used to the familiarity of the two voices outside of the belly, and they're dreaming of that initial introduction.

Packing for Three—The All Important Hospital Bag

Now that you know what to expect for the last leg of pregnancy, you want to make the hospital experience as relaxed as possible by prepping everyone's hospital overnight bag. Having everything needed for the mother, child, and you can save you a lot of time and worry. You can trust that leaving the hospital to secure more items is the opposite joy. So, take notes and start getting ready to pack for the most anticipated trip of the year.

Don't pack alone and don't do it without a checklist. Some items might slip your mind or your partner's mind, so gather a list and cross things off as you go. Don't be afraid to ask the experts what they took to the hospital for delivery. Every active mother and father knows necessary hospital bag items to take that won't be on your list. Also, don't attempt to fit everything into one bag. It will be easier to locate a person's specifics if they have their own bag. Pack two bags for your partner, one for you, and one for the baby. There have been times when the mother-to-be is already at the hospital for an appointment or something happened and she drove herself or someone else due to potential labor. That extra bag in her car with the same items will come in handy and save you time and stress. It's a good thought to have all bags packed a few months before the potential due date. An unexpected delivery will make you wish you had packed early.

The hospital bag for mom will contain the most, and that's even if you mistakenly pack one. Print off multiple copies of the detailed and finished birth plan you discussed, and keep several copies in each of the mom's bags. Passing out the birth plan to the delivery team will ensure that everyone is on the same page as the parents. It helps should any last-minute questions arise or if the two of you failed to go over the plan at previous appointments.

There isn't a definition for the word labor that describes it as being easy. Labor is in fact difficult, and it could last a long time. You should expect your time at the hospital to last hours before the delivery happens, but keep in mind that it may take even longer. Unless already specified, your significant other won't have to remain in bed until she pushes out the baby. The nurses will encourage you to walk with her around the room, hallway, or hospital grounds. Pacing is an excellent way to pass the time, but do it in style and comfort. Pack the plush bathrobe, memory foam slippers, and thick socks. The robe serves as walking attire and loungewear. The slippers are a must for strolling around or using the restroom. Those socks will keep her feet warm in that freezing hospital room.

She will want to be able to pass the time in between the moments of pain and stress. The hospital room might have a television, but you can't be too sure about the extras it might contain. Bring a tablet or laptop and see about making sure her cellphone has a mobile hotspot. Access to her favorite show or movies will make for an enjoyable time. Speaking of cellphones, don't forget her charger. Other technological items to bring include headphones or earbuds and a Bluetooth speaker.

Mom will also need a list of items to have for after the delivery. Shower shoes or flip-flops are a must for any shower outside of your house. Heavy bleeding is common after having a baby, so pack those pads. Ask your partner what kind she needs because an extra heavy pad will likely be in order. Toss in several pairs of underwear that have enough fabric to support a pad so don't be silly and pack thongs or other thin underwear. She's going to nurse in the hospital if the choice was to take the breastfeeding route. A few nursing bras will be a matter of convenience. Her personal sleepwear will be preferred over the traditional hospital gown complete with a drafty open back; however, since your partner's strength will be questionable, it's a good idea to opt for the at-home nightgown over pants and a sleep shirt. It will make the difficult bathroom trips easier.

Other essentials include daily toiletries like deodorant, moisturizer, toothpaste and toothbrush, nightcaps, and more, and also bring a few changes of clothes. Basically, you want to make sure your partner has everything to use in the hospital that they could use at home.

Your dad bag will contain most of the same items as the mom bag. A few exceptions include your razor and a possible camera. Shaving is part of your daily routine, but to even shower at all in the hospital room requires permission from the hospital. They usually don't care. The staff understands that you are also emotionally and physically spent, and a good shower might be refreshing. As for the camera, you have a phone capable of taking quality photos, but a good camera adds a special touch for creating life-long memories.

Your child's bag is special and full of tiny items. Newborns can struggle to regulate body temperature, so pack booties and socks to help keep them snug. Pack a blanket to go along with the hospital blanket used to swaddle your baby after delivery. Your blanket can add extra warmth in the room and on the way home from the hospital. A special outfit to wear home should also be a priority. Dress for the weather, but make sure your baby stands out from the rest. He or she will look awesome in the stylish car seat that's already waiting to be used in your vehicle.

Plan Your Route

The only thing left is to plug the hospital's address into your device for easy traveling. Do a practice drive during different hours of the day to get used to what the time of travel would be like. The labor and delivery department should also be listed in your favorites along with your OB or midwife. You want to notify the hospital and your OB or midwife that your spouse or girlfriend is on the way.

Chapter 5:

Preparation

You've sat around with your buddies who are already living life in the parenting world. They deliver detail after detail about what you need to buy to get yourself and your house ready to handle the little bundle of joy that is getting ready to invade your life. The stories are wonderful, funny, scary, and sometimes confusing. Like, why would you need to inspect house plants? Don't worry, we'll cover that too. Prepping doesn't only consist of buying items for ensuring your house is fit, you have to prepare yourself physically, mentally, and emotionally. The dos and don'ts of baby planning carry a lot of weight, but that's why you're here to learn.

Outside of your closest friends, you can lean on your family for parenthood education and emotional support. If you're lucky, you still have your parents to go to, and they are more than willing to offer up some old-school advice. Parents have a magical way of giving you the goods as if they've been in your shoes before. Perhaps you should soak up some of that knowledge. Siblings who have dipped their toes into the parenting waters are sometimes great teachers as well. Whoever you go to for advice or if people offer it up unsolicited, pick it apart and gather the best details to help guide you to safe decision making.

The easiest decision you can make by far is to move toward a healthier lifestyle. You have obviously done a great job making sure your partner stopped all of the bad habits she enjoyed pre-

pregnancy. Now, how about taking care of your body. You want to be around to help raise your child. The months and years will turn into countless moments of firsts, and it would be a shame for you to miss out on those because health didn't become a priority.

Health is vital for you, but did you know that your good or bad health could help determine the baby's physical state at the time of conception? According to OB/GYN, Joseph Garza, the vigor of a man's sperm is equal to the healthiness of a woman's egg (Oakley, 2014). If planning for pregnancy came first, then start improving yourself if conception hasn't happened at this point in your reading. Some studies suggest that men who are overweight, consume high-fat foods, or suffer from diabetes have a higher risk of producing a baby who is more likely to be obese. Not having the healthiest standards at the time of pregnancy shouldn't keep you from taking the next step in becoming the best father in terms of physicality.

Do you have pets? There's a good chance that you might be home before the evening gets too long. If you have a dog, they should be okay waiting until you make it home to go relieve themselves. The problem is, a good chance doesn't equal a great one. You might not make it home until the next day or later. The process of pregnancy is unpredictable. There are stories of people who go in for a routine appointment and end up staying because it's time to deliver the baby. Those emergency deliveries could keep the father out of the house for multiple days, so what do you do if you have pets? It's too much stress to run home and take care of them. You might make it home once to grab a few things, but if you have that hospital bag in your vehicle, there's no need. The dog has to go outside multiple times per day. Feedings occur multiple times. You have to have a plan in place to take care of your animals. Find someone you can trust earlier in the pregnancy to help you out should delivery arrive sooner than expected. Give them a key to your place and a list of how much food a specific animal gets. It's probably important to introduce the person to the animal(s) months in advance. The idea is to get your pet(s) used to someone they might typically think is a stranger. Walk them through the schedule of walks, bathroom usage, feedings, medicine, treats, and anything else that might be on the list. If necessary, have the person handle things for a few days or so before the delivery. This person will probably help you with your pets free of charge considering what it's for; however, you are thankful that someone stepped in and you are more than willing to make sure they receive payment.

Feeding, Sleeping, and Style

Have you had discussions with your significant other about how the two of you are going to parent your child? Chances are that she was raised differently than you were, and the both of you have pros and cons from what you know about how you were each raised from birth. Attachment is a security that the baby relies on from the start. They need to know the parents are going to come through with a consistent schedule. Pay attention and equip yourself with essential subject matter to start a conversation with your partner.

Are you guys planning to implement breastfeeding or bottle feeding? Babies deal with a lot while adjusting to life outside of the womb, and breast milk can help the baby fight off various infections. Some benefits of nursing include:

- Prevent diarrhea
- Prevent ear infections
- Aids in digestion

47

- Increases bond with mom through skin-to-skin contact
- It's free

The nursing experience isn't always the best option. Many mothers have experienced painful difficulties during the process, and they would rather not continue. Sometimes, stories from women who have traveled this road turn new mothers off from even attempting to nurse. Other cons to breastfeeding have to do with time restraints. Feedings may occur every few hours when mother's milk is involved, and a mother who plans on going back to work doesn't always want to pump at the office or the stay-at-home mom may want that extra time to rest or run the day-to day-errands. In some cases, even if the mom really wants to breastfeed, the baby may not take to it.

Opting for formula is convenient when you and the mother need to drop off the little one or if you are taking on nightly feeding duties. Yes, the mother can store her breast milk for you or a caregiver to bottle up later. The problem is, what's the point of you helping to feed at night if your partner is around? Chances are that her breasts are filled up and ready to go when the baby is ready to eat. If formula feeding happens from the start, your partner's ducts will dry up, and she won't need to pump throughout the day. Another plus of formula is that babies don't need as much because it's not as easy to digest. This allows for more rest for you, mom, and baby. The cons? Formula is rather expensive. Costs can add up to $1,500 the first year in the United States alone. Prices are cheaper in the UK but soar up in countries like China. Formula isn't where the money spending ends. Be prepared to buy bottles, nipples, cleaning tools, warmers, and insulated bottle carriers. Feedings aren't an area where you can save money if you choose formula.

There isn't always a right choice when deciding how baby feeding is going to go. The mother might decide to go in the opposite direction after the child enters the world; however, having the conversation will help you check an essential item off of your preparation list. Don't worry about possibly buying supplies and them not getting used. You will need bottles no matter what. How much is what might change.

Babies cry and eat quite often. If you're wondering when they actually sleep after hearing about the potential feedings every few hours, the short answer is eventually. Yes, of course your child is going to sleep, and you and the mother will appreciate all seconds, minutes, and if you're lucky, hours the baby sleeps. Where and how will the newborn rest when they close their eyes?

There are different studies that suggest a timetable for when your baby should start vacationing in their own room. Most agree that it shouldn't happen before four months. Some suggest you can wait until nine months or longer. The decision falls on the parents, and it might change depending on how much rest the adults are getting by sharing a space with the baby, but it's best to hold off on placing the baby in their own room until it's safer to do so.

Discussions about parenting styles should start when two people decide to move past the dating stage in their relationship. You want to know that your potential life partner is on the same page as you when it comes to building a life together. The decision on whether or not you want kids is only the starting point. The conversation continues even into your child's adult years. How many kids do you want? Pampers or Huggies? Are you doing childcare or will one of you transition to a stay-at-home parent? Yes, gone are the days when the mother leaves her job to raise the kids. It's a decision that carries much weight, and more men are the ones making that transition.

You're reading this book, so commitment is already the standard for you, but having an open dialogue about parenting expectations will continue to strengthen the foundation between you and your partner. Adding kids to the mix won't strain your relationship, but it will rearrange your idea of normal. If the two of you don't find common ground on how to raise your child, it will lead to unnecessary arguments.

The first issue to address is late-night feedings. Look, one thing you can tip your hat on is your baby will not sleep all night long. Don't expect your significant other to handle the responsibility alone. Discuss a strategy that will make sense for both parties. Getting up in the middle of the night will never feel gratifying but knowing you are trading off with someone who has your back will go a long way in bonding as one. The most successful parents are the ones who know they're in it together whether it's the happy babyface moments or the crying without end segments. Those crying moments can put you into a spell. Sometimes nothing is working. The baby isn't hungry, their diaper is dry, and rocking them does little to nothing for soothing. Perhaps you want to plug their mouth with a pacifier. Well, what if that's not something the mother does during her alone time with the newborn? Too many parents use the pacifier as a quick fix solution. The sucking motion is something a baby starts getting used to in the womb. It's soothing, to say the least, but it also creates an expectation. What if your baby is used to falling asleep with a pacifier in their mouth, but one of the parents doesn't use that method? You get an infant who is confused about what they need. There are pros and cons to using a pacifier but decide together if it's the right answer for your parenting style.

Buying and Stocking the House

Nine months is a long time. There are seasons, work projects, holidays, and hopefully vacations. You work hard to make sure your money can go toward having fun and securing a future. Guess what? You're no longer the normal guy living for yourself, and bringing a child into the world means less time to maximize your savings. Dads will always have more and more items to add to their child's life and it starts before the baby takes their first breath. Take advantage of a nine-month warning and start buying for the baby early so you don't get hit with the costs all at once. Below is the list of things to buy and stock up on in preparation for adding a baby to your life.

The most important thing from the moment the pregnancy is confirmed is to start making sure your partner is ready to have a healthy pregnancy. Prenatal vitamins put the essential needs into the body to help with healthy development. The vitamins help make up for the nutrients missing due to potential morning sickness or a picky diet. A prescription for vitamins might run you up to $60 per month. An over-the-counter option will cost much less. Other items to purchase for your partner include a body pillow and belly butter for stretch marks.

You already know it will be four to nine months before the baby moves into their rent-free room. The good news is that buying a bed can wait. Even when your little one moves into their space, they will be too small to have a bed. But, they need a comfortable resting place for bedtime and naps. You will notice the mother will cuddle with and fall asleep with the baby in your bed. It happens quite often during the late night and early morning feeding times, so prepare your wallet for a bassinet and crib. A bassinet is the first sleeping arrangement for your newborn. The small, oval-shaped bed unit will keep your baby comfortable from the time you bring them home up to four months. It's easy to move a bassinet around, so you can transport it between the bedroom or living room. For instance, if your wife or girlfriend had to have a C-section, then it might be a strain for them to move up and down the stairs. Some mothers have opted to use a comfortable couch, futon, or daybed while recovering from a Cesarean procedure. Having a bassinet nearby provides comfort while getting up to take care of the baby. A good, reliable bassinet could cost right over $100 or more. You'll want to have a crib to use once the baby is too long or heavy for the bassinet. You might think you have more time before making that purchase since the baby can stay put for at least the first four months, but don't fall for that trap. You'll want to have the crib together before you come home from the hospital, so purchase it early in the pregnancy. Cribs can be anywhere from $200 to well over $450 for the higher-end models.

An infant carrier or all exclusive car seats are next up. The carrier usually lasts up to the first year of the child's life before upgrading. If you plan it correctly, the seat can be purchased along with the new stroller. The base of the car seat stays in your car, while the seat itself goes back and forth between the vehicle and the stroller. Some car seats are also made to fit specific car models or baby sizes. Because the car seat serves to protect your child, you want to do your job and find the best fit for comfort, style, and safety. Price comes down to what you're willing to pay, but you don't want to cut any corners when it comes to your child. Good strollers run from $400 to over $1,000 depending on the model.

Another item to purchase while waiting for your child to arrive is a changing table. The changing table serves as an area to change diapers, wipe your baby's soiled area, and get the baby dressed. You lay your baby on top of the changing area and use the attached strap or seat belt holder to keep your child in place. Don't ever leave the area while your baby is on top of the table. It only takes a few seconds for them to flip over and fall off of the table. The drop is only a few feet high, but that's enough to do some damage, especially to the not yet developed skull. The great thing about most changing tables is that they also serve as a storage area. Most parents place their extra baby wipes, diapers, powder, butt paste, and onesies on the shelves or inside the cabinet area of the changing tables. You'll want to buy something that's going to last. A good changing table with proper storage can cost anywhere from $100 to $500 depending on where you're looking.

Don't forget that all-important baby monitor. When looking at baby monitors, don't consider saving a few bucks by getting the simple walky-talky style noise monitors. It's time to splurge on a video monitor. With a non-video option, you are constantly getting up and checking on the baby with every fuss and whimper you hear. You run the risk of accidentally alerting your little one to your presence when they would've been perfectly fine with waiting it out. If you have a video monitor, you can easily check to see what the baby is doing. Often enough, those sounds are from the dream your infant is experiencing. Viewing before going to look in on the bundle of joy is an ideal situation.

A great tip for purchasing diapers is to know they come in different sizes and your baby can outgrow them faster than you'd think. Preemie and newborn diapers are the sizes that you would use least of all. It's hard determining how long your infant will be in each size, so it's better to start with a newborn size and size one diaper of a few different brands. Depending on the company, your baby might react differently to the material around their waist, or it's possible the diaper could leak. Once you know what brand is best, you can stock up on different sizes. You can even purchase baby wipes that match the diaper brand. Make sure they are fragrance-free and buy them in bulk. You can never have too many baby wipes.

Getting items for the baby is great, but don't forget about filling your house with future time savers. Life after bringing the baby home will not allow for the day-to-day moments of grocery shopping and errand running. Load up on extra pet food for those days when your cat or dog is waiting by an empty food bowl because you were too tired to remember to add their food to your list. Buying extra essentials is also key. Laundry soap, dryer sheets, dish soap, toilet paper, toothpaste, and deodorant are other must-have items. Making those purchases will make life easier once you're in parenting mode. Stock up on pantry, refrigerator, and freezer items too. Focus on quick and easy to cook items because fighting through a fog of sleep to prepare a meal won't be something you're too interested in doing.

Chapter 6:

The Day Has Come

The mother-to-be's overnight bag is in your trunk, and there's another one in hers because you're prepared. It's either morning, afternoon, evening, or the middle of the night. The OB or midwife is on speed dial, and they are finally convinced that Braxton Hicks (false labor pains) have made way for the real thing. Holy crap! The time has come to say hello to your child. Did you lock the doors? You called her mother, but did you call yours? Oh no, did you drive to the hospital without your pregnant partner? It feels like everything you worked toward over the last nine months is making a plan of its own. The moment is overwhelming, but press pause on panic. You're feeling what every other dad has felt at one time or another. Here's a secret, the moms also go through these moments of anxiety. You got this! Don't forget that you have prepared for this moment. Everything you learned from the birthing classes will make the chaotic moments more peaceful. You are sharing this experience with the mother and that already increases the potential for a safe and positive outcome. Women who have support during the delivery are known to go through shorter hours of labor.

Although short deliveries tend to happen, it isn't something you should necessarily expect, nor should you be surprised if the arrival date doesn't match the expected delivery date. One thing about babies is that they like to make an entrance. They enjoy reminding the parents that it's their show. You've seen the television shows or movies where the non-doctor has to

55

deliver the newborn while stuck in traffic. Sometimes they show the mother in labor for double-digit hours. You've even occasionally heard instances where drugs aren't wanted, but alarming screams later indicate that the epidural has been requested. The thrown-in wrench is all part of the learning process. This is why you've asked the questions, listened to the accounts from established parents, taken the classes, and gone to the appointments. So, whether the ride is smooth on this day or it's an emergency cesarean, you are by your partner's side to reassure her that it's going to be okay.

No, Really, the Day Has Come

Let's break it all down a bit more to understand the moments of labor. There's no such thing as being over-prepared in the baby game. Labor actually has three stages, and knowing the details makes it easier on you. Before we dive in, remember your partner isn't going to have the same fun time her mother had during labor or that cashier, Beth, from the grocery store. Remind your lovely girl that her pregnancy is uniquely fitted for her.

The first stage of labor is a trickster because it has three parts. There's the early phase, active phase, and transition phase. Early isn't short. This phase lasts for 12 special hours, but the good news is that time is reduced after the first pregnancy. The active phase is only six hours long (sometimes less), but the contractions are harder. This is the part from before when you don't wait for a decision. You're on your way to the medical center with the mother. Here is when those drug-free delivery decisions might reverse. Don't make the mother feel bad about changing her mind, and take it easy on yourself. If your hope for an all-natural birth has gone away, you can take comfort in knowing that an epidural or other pain medications are proven to be safe for the mother and child. Instead of worrying about the pain, you can help her alleviate some by utilizing the breathing methods learned from class. The transition phase arrives with the impact of 60–90 second contractions, and they aren't light. A lucky individual only suffers this phase for a few minutes, but they are known to last for a few plus hours.

The second stage of labor is more intense than the first. Sure, the first stage is hours long, sometimes going into the next day, but now it's time for the mother-to-be to put in work that drains her physically, mentally, and emotionally. Hold her hand and let her squeeze yours as hard as she has to. This is the moment when she, who has been doing the majority of the yelling, gets screamed at herself. Orders for her to push and breathe take center stage.

The third stage of labor gets its cue from the baby. Once that bundle is secure, it's time to deliver the placenta. The placenta is an organ that has kept your baby alive on the inside. It takes away waste from the child's blood while providing the necessary nutrients and oxygen for the fetus to survive. The mother's body is spent from the hardships of the first delivery. Make sure you stay with her for the second one. She needs you for strength and to let her know the miracle you created together is safe.

Here is a checklist of tell-tell signs that you're about to move from inactive father to active father.

- Contractions (tightening the muscles of the uterus) are intense and more frequent
- The cervix starts to dilate (opens to 10 centimeters for most pregnancies for the baby to pass through)

- Bloody show (increased vaginal discharge that is thick and pinkish)
- Increased back pain and cramps
- Diarrhea
- Water breaks (it's when the amniotic sac around the fetus releases fluid)

She can endure contractions, and the water never breaks on its own. There's also a chance for the sac to burst, but labor doesn't start. In that case, be ready to have the hospital induce labor to avoid infection. Induced labor is when methods (pharmaceutical or non-pharmaceutical) are used to start the labor process.

Don't rush your partner. Pay attention to the signs and communicate with the person charged with the delivery before speeding to the hospital. Labor typically starts at home, and it continues there for hours. Why speed to the hospital when the two of you can be comfortable at home? You'll often find that many parents jump into action and end up at the hospital hours before the doctor shows up. The OB or midwife typically doesn't make it to labor and delivery until they know their services are needed. Women have gone to the hospital in the morning only to get sent home and return that night or the next morning. The doctors aren't going to sit around for the duration of a lengthy labor. The cervix dilates 3–6 centimeters during the early stages of labor, and that can last up to 12 hours.

What should you do at home? If she's up to moving around, suggest going for a walk in the neighborhood. Really, it's not a bad idea because there is time to waste as you wait. Your partner might be exhausted. The strain from the pain is taking a toll, and the worry is mounting up. It's okay for her to nap if the baby allows her to do so. Do whatever you can to help her relax. Seriously, turn on the TV and have a Netflix and chill (seriously, chill) moment.

You can time the contractions while at home, but be easy on the timing. Constantly running the numbers will make both of you think she's in labor when she's not or that the labor is longer than it is. She's in early labor if the pain is steady and lasts for 30 seconds or more. Early labor is an indicator to contact the midwife or OB. Give them the specifics and wait for a decision. The professionals usually know when you should bring your significant other in and when you should not. If you notice the contractions are five minutes apart or less, hit for 30 seconds or more, and repeat that pattern for an hour, you don't need to wait for a decision. In that scenario, labor has decided it's time to get to a hospital bed, and waiting to call the doctor for a decision is a waste of time.

According to a Change of Plans

There are different birth plans for different parents. In a perfect world, you and the baby's mother have every detail figured out down to whether or not she's wearing hospital socks or bringing her own pair. It's great to be ready, and you should be proud that you've made it this far. This book isn't meant to put more pressure on you, so try to understand that during this part of the reading. You have lived long enough to know life doesn't care about your plans. Emergencies take center stage at a moment's notice. Even emergencies come with their own set of rules. Some are big and some are small, but they all matter to the people they affect.

Most importantly, your role in the delivery room doesn't change. The mother-to-be needs your support. You are the nurse when it's only the two of you in the room. Continue to put her comfort first and alert the real nurse if matters worsen. You are also her coach and cheerleader. Even as the plan changes, you must be a source of security and comfort. You got this. Preparing to help in labor and delivery is something you've been waiting for forever since you found out about the pregnancy. You had an energy bar, plenty of water, and now you're good to go.

We already discussed how easily the choice of taking an epidural versus an all-natural delivery can change. Understanding your partner's wants is key before she even goes into labor. The intensity of labor could wash away every bit of planning your significant other had, and it's up to you to advocate for her when the brain fog sets in. Remind her of expressed wishes when violent shouts seem to take over the original plan. It's a good idea to go ahead and share those same wishes with the delivery team before things get too deep. They may attempt to do their best to follow the outline if the delivery is safe.

Well, more serious items might come into play. A vaginal delivery was the ideal choice, but the odds have shifted toward a C-section. Cesareans happen in 33% of pregnancies, but first-time mothers experience them less than 15% of the time (Gregory, n.d.). If a C-section is necessary, you can still be at your partner's side during the procedure. If the decision is made weeks out, then the safety increases, and the move was made for precautionary reasons; however, an emergency C-section involves more risks. Blood pressure, bleeding, or other reasons might prohibit the mother-to-be from making the decision or even discussing it with you and the delivery team. What's your choice going to be? Have this trying conversation with your partner throughout the pregnancy. Her thoughts and yours might change depending on what trimester she's in. In the most extreme cases, the decision might come down to choosing between the mother and child. It's never an ideal situation, and hopefully, the discussion never has to move past the conversation stage for anyone reading this guide.

The Real Fun Starts

Your child is breathing fresh air, testing out those lungs, and placing a smile on each face they come across. Congratulations to you for the growth you've achieved over the past nine months. No longer will you be considered a dad-to-be. In truth, everything you have done to support your partner and learn about your baby already made you a dad. Make sure you say a thank you to the delivery team and don't forget to kiss the infant's mother.

What's next now that the short or long delivery has taken place? Daddy protocol dictates that you get to cut the umbilical cord—an honor worthy of any king. In the United States, the nurses will stamp the bottom of the child's feet to press on the birth certificate, and some hospitals ask the father if they want the prints pressed against a shirt or towel as a keepsake. If the baby is going to a nursery or neonatal or newborn intensive care unit (NICU), you are more than welcome to join them. Your infant will appreciate the time, and you can start bonding with them. You've discussed skin-to-skin contact with your significant other throughout the pregnancy. Chances are that you get to witness it firsthand with the mom; however, if the mother isn't in a position to start the bond, you can start for her. The emotional benefits are worth the touch. The baby will enjoy better brain development, cry less often, and experience better breathing and sleeping. Those are only some of the ways skin-to-skin contact is successful.

Have you changed a real diaper before? Well, you can get started while in the hospital. The nurses are more than willing to teach a first-time father the proper techniques of diaper changing. There's a specific way to wipe your daughter, and you'll learn that cold air will cause your son to make it rain upward. Enjoy it. You never forget your first diaper.

Breastfeeding is another area of fun to explore at the hospital. Take the time to appreciate that forming bond between the two most important people in your life. Is the moment proving to be difficult for the mother and child? Not only is it fine, but it's common as well. Talk to the midwife or OB about ways you can help with building healthy breastfeeding for your family. That skin-to-skin contact we talked about bridges the gap between mother and child for successful feeding times. You can bring the baby to their tired mother when it's time for a meal.

You're not going to want to stop watching your child, even when they are sleeping, but don't forget that you are the connection to the outside world after the delivery is complete. Go into the waiting area and share the good news with the folks out there. Make those phone calls to spread the joy from coast to coast or across the pond. Families like sending out birth announcements. Take a picture of your swaddled infant to use for creating that shared memory.

If all went well, you can expect to leave the hospital within one to two days. That first drive with your newborn is quite scary. All of a sudden, the other drivers worry you like never before. You're already a good dad, and you'll get your family home safe.

Chapter 7:

The First Three Months

Life starts again for the first time. You and your partner arrived home from the hospital with your precious bundle of joy. Happy doesn't accurately describe your feelings. Your entire world has changed, and it's time to start making memories as a new family. But wait, you notice that the new mother and baby seem exhausted, and you're right there with them. Sleep is one of the most important aspects of successful parenting. A restless infant leads to irritable and unhealthy parents. You could play the hero to the mother and take care of your precious bundle when they wake up in an untimely manner, but then your sacrifice limits your energy and concentration throughout the day. How can you be the best father if you're hurting physically and mentally? You can't. A child needs two parents working at their best to properly care for him or her. Don't feel upset about making your mental and physical stability a priority.

You now see that rest is the way for you to perform at your best. That's great because understanding, motivation, focus, and love are what it's going to take to start your baby off right. Look at the first few weeks as an extension of the pregnancy. It sounds weird, especially since your partner has pulled off the delivery. The last thing you want to do is make her think she's still pregnant, but babies aren't ready for the world in the same way other baby mammals are. It's good to manipulate their new environment to mimic life inside the womb. The baby is still used to the barrier created in the womb, which had made them accustomed to constant touch and the sounds of the mother's heartbeat, so part of the moments of irritation and untimely crying has more to do with the newborn missing the life they had for nine months.

It's possible that your partner doesn't know about the "recreating the womb" theory. Go ahead and impress her with this newly acquired knowledge. It benefits her as much as helping the baby adjust to the new world. Mom can use wraps, slings, and carriers to "wear their baby" as an extension of the pregnancy. This action frees the mother up to do as little as possible at home. The process allows your partner to heal physically and emotionally. Delivery is hard on the body, especially a C-section. Tearing and bleeding may occur, and handling the baby too much could cause a strain in the surgical area. Postpartum could be emotionally affecting the mother. "Recreating the womb" could ease the mood swings associated with postpartum depression. Strapping the baby close to the mother during the day invites moments of extra sleep for the child, and time to regain energy for the mother.

The crying can become intense. Your partner is suffering from it, and those tears are working your last nerve. It's not always easy to pinpoint the source of your child's distress. The mother has tried feeding the little one from both breasts, but it results in the child detaching, throwing their head back, and screaming uncontrollably. The continual process is a back and forth with mom pleading with the baby for information as to what is wrong. Depression is setting in, and you step up to take control of the situation. You aren't able to get down to discover your child's reason for discomfort either. They won't take the bottle and holding them doesn't bring comfort. Anger and frustration are taking over both parents. What do you do? Place the baby in the bassinet or crib and walk away for a bit. Many parents have shaken their babies out of frustration and in an effort to calm the noise. DO NOT DO THIS. Shaken baby syndrome is a form of abuse that brings head trauma that may lead to significant brain damage or death.

Expect your baby to need that extra love and attention for the next 12 weeks, which means creating the same sensations of the womb on the outside is crucial to their development. It's not an easy job, but it helps, and you and the mother will see how fast your child responds and hits those cognitive and physical benchmarks.

It's a good time to explain to the soon-to-be visitors how you want life to go now that the baby is home. You, the mother, and the baby need as much quiet time as possible. Not to mention, you want the time to bond as a family. Many new dads place a sign on the front door that mentions there's a new baby in the house. What does that mean? It's usually a sign that you don't want people unnecessarily ringing the doorbell or knocking too loud. A great way to ease the tension between your house and potential guests (relatives and family friends) is to do birth announcements. A timely announcement with a great baby photo will go a long way in showing off the baby without a personal introduction. You can mail them off to your older relatives, but to save time and money, those birth announcements can be uploaded to social media. All of your friends and family can meet your child in a digital manner. Since living in a world with COVID, everyone has had to adapt, which means almost everyone you know is familiar with Zoom, Teams, or some other alternative for video calling. You can share the big news and have your family meet their newest relative. Doing so will protect your baby's compromised immune system.

Baby Development and Milestones

Communication with your baby starts right away, which is one of the first steps to positive baby development. You won't know what they want initially, and quite often, the mother knows what's wrong before you. Don't feel discouraged. Mother and child have a bond that you don't. After all, your partner built a unique connection over nine months that wins out all of the time. Your newborn knows who you are, and they are trying to let you know what they need. Babies usually have needs that fit into three general categories that illustrate their distinctive personality. Those categories include peaceful, urgent, and unknown. A peaceful baby is sleeping well, playing by themselves, and isn't in need of any basic care. You'll glance from around the corner and notice them kicking their legs with excitement, following objects with their eyes, and making those cute baby sounds. Don't disturb them in these moments. Peaceful babies are working on self-soothing. It gives you an opportunity to sit or work on something quietly. An urgent baby can bring momentary stress to your life, but it is quickly resolved once you figure out the cause. Your newborn utilizes their skills of whimpering, body agitation, and screaming to show you they want food, need a diaper change, or want to connect by being held or rocked. Their cries even sound different depending on the specific need. You'll become a pro at deciphering the tones of those sounds. The trickiest category to deal with is the unknown. The number one problem with the unknown is that it's a mystery to the infant as well. He or she doesn't need or want the typical problems solved, and trying to do so only irritates them more. Behavior becomes erratic as they move between the calm and the storm at a moment's notice. Here is where you go into your toolbag and do every and anything to bring joy back to the child's life. Singing, being held outside, or going for a drive might do the trick. Sometimes they'll surprise you by letting their cries solve the mysterious problem.

Other communication milestones include turning the head, coos and smiles, responding to sounds and voices, and making eye contact. Your baby has done a great job strengthening those neck muscles and turning their head to demonstrate a specific response. Make sure you're properly supporting the head when holding your child. He or she may violently whip their head in response to their mother's voice, and the same will happen when you enter the room as mom holds them. The sound of a parent's voice also causes them to smile. You'll notice that your newborn smiles more when you or your spouse or girlfriend is around. That's a good sign. It means the baby is comfortable and feels protected around you. Other sounds might cause a different reaction. Your baby might get quiet at the sound of a barking dog, music playing, or an unfamiliar voice. Their curiosity causes them to focus on the source of the noise, or they're determining whether or not they like the new sound. Eye contact is essential for the baby's social, emotional, and brain development. They're gaining an understanding of social human interaction. Smiles are the same. In the beginning, eye contact and smiling are natural, but they aren't doing it on a conscious level. After the first month, smiling and eye contact are all about connecting on a social level. Your baby will smile to get you to smile back. By three months, your baby should consistently perform at these visual and hearing levels.

- Begins to gain coordination with hands and eyes
- Babbles
- Starts to imitate sounds
- Watches faces intently

- Regularly smiles at the sound of the parents' voice
- Turns toward sound
- Can recognize familiar people or things at a greater distance

Sensory development is crucial for positive baby development. Their surroundings (mostly your house) have much input when it comes to developing sensory skills. Outside of the parent's voices, jiggly movements, and the mother's heartbeat, many feelings, sounds, and movements are unfamiliar to a newborn. You will notice your baby taking the first three months to develop sensory skills to adapt to and interact with the environment outside the womb. It's exciting to see this growth. By three months, your baby should easily experience these sensory skills.

- Calming from touch, sound, and rocking
- Track objects with side-to-side head and eye movement while on their back
- Keep their head in place as they focus on objects while on their back
- Reaching for a toy while on their back
- Enjoy happy moments like rocking, bouncing, and swaying

Motor skills development increases rapidly during the first three months as well. Motor skill training occurs almost instantly. It's something that your baby will work hard on developing each day, but, of course, you will want to help stimulate this activity. Sleeping is one of the ways infants increase motor skills, and once again, you can help with this process. It's tempting to lay the baby in the crib or bassinet in a position where they get their best rest, but doing so limits motor development. Try positioning the head differently from time to time, that way your baby is encouraged to move their head around to build up the muscles in the head and neck. Look out for these motor skill milestones by three months.

- While on their stomach, they lift and hold their head up
- While on their stomach, they use arms to push up
- While on their stomach or back, they stretch out their legs and begin to kick
- Swipes at hanging objects
- Grasps or shakes hands or small hand toys
- Brings their hand to their mouth

You'll get encouraged by your baby's improved motor skills, but don't allow your excitement to have them testing out those skills when sleeping should be happening. It's dangerous to lay your infant on their stomach during a nap or bedtime. A key way to remember what to do is to memorize: back to sleep, tummy to play. Your little one might tucker themselves out during tummy playtime. That's okay. Simply position them to their back and allow rest to take place.

Baby's Medical Needs

Going home from the hospital is wonderful, but those first three months aren't doctor-free time for your new family. There's a schedule to follow for making routine appointments for checkups and immunizations, but those aren't the only times your baby will be seen. How often should you be taking your child to a medical professional? The answer is whenever it's necessary.

Scheduled checkups do help reduce the need to take your baby in at random times. Those child wellness appointments help look for anything that may be wrong based on regular development and milestones. Missing a scheduled visit could cause a problem to linger more than it should have.

The scheduling and timetable for infant visits depend on the doctor or medical facility. A small suburban doctor's office probably handles these checkups much differently than a military base. Some doctors are more detailed with their timely examinations, while others are more relaxed, so they spread the appointments out. A more recent change in appointment scheduling could be due to COVID pandemic protocols based on country location. The first typical birth to three months baby checkup happens before leaving the hospital. The newborn checkup happens throughout the hospital stay three or more times. The medical team has to make sure the baby is fit to go home. The newborn tests consist of the following.

- Blood tests following the birth
- Hearing screenings
    - Otoacoustic Emissions Test (OAE)
    - Auditory BrainStem Response (ABR)

For the blood tests, the nurse pricks the heel of your baby's foot to collect the sample. Prepare yourself because it's hard to see your baby experience pain for the first time. The blood sample goes to the lab for testing. The lab screens the blood for 30 disorders to see if your child contains any of them. The testing is important as it alerts the doctors to any serious problems. Early detection allows for swift action to put a treatment plan in place. The pain lasts for a few minutes, but it's worth the tears.

The hearing test is quick and painless. Your baby's medical team will most likely perform two tests to check for any issues in the ears that pertain to potential hearing loss. The tests are highly reliable and can detect issues with hearing right from birth.

The OAE is one of the hearing tests medical professionals use. They place a small microphone and earphone in your baby's ear. The earphones send out sound to test the hearing. If there aren't any issues, sound from the speaker echo through the microphone.

The ABR uses two earphones to deliver sound straight to the child's ear. The team attaches electrodes to the baby's head to detect neural stimulation from the auditory brain stem. The electrodes light up if a proper connection from the ear to the brain is detected. A spotty connection or zero connection is an indicator of hearing loss.

Administering the first dose of the HepB vaccine before the baby goes home is another thing done by most hospitals. The shot should take place within 24 hours of birth. The HepB vaccine protects the baby from contracting hepatitis B from any family members who unknowingly have the disease.

The first visit after leaving the hospital occurs in three to five days. You and your partner are probably worn out, but it's important to keep your appointment. These initial checkups allow the doctor to see if everything is taking place for your baby to thrive, and if not, steps will be put in place to address any issues. The doctor will do a physical exam to cover weight, height, and head circumference, which will be typical for all appointments; however, this first visit will cover a few things that won't be necessary later.

- The umbilical cord hasn't completely fallen off, but the doctor can detect if the tissue around the stumped area is healing according to plan.

- Jaundice doesn't occur as frequently as in the past, but it is something that may affect your newborn. The yellow tint to the skin is caused by the body's difficulties in removing old red blood cells. You might have seen pictures or videos of babies who have jaundice. It isn't anything for you to worry about. Doctors look for jaundice early and can fix the problem without any trouble.

- Circumcision is another item to check at the first appointment, but, of course, that's only if your baby is a boy and you and your partner have agreed to have a circumcision done.

The two-week checkup is standard with hardly any red flags. Don't be alarmed if your baby lost some of their birth weight during the first week, it's normal; however, that weight should have been gained back by the two-week appointment. The physical exam doesn't go beyond the basics for weight, height, and head circumference. Also, don't expect your baby to receive any immunizations at the first two appointments. If anything, monitor your child's sleeping and eating habits or schedule and deliver that information to the nurse and doctor. They may notice anything that doesn't add up.

There is also a one and two-month visit. The one-month checkup is similar to the others with the exception of a possible HepB second dose. Outside of that, the only big points are

72

how your baby is growing. Now, the two-month visit is the one babies would fear if they knew what was waiting at the doctor's office. Parents don't anticipate taking their little one to the two-month checkup. Sure, you have good news to share with the nurses and doctors. Your precious little one has started coming into their own at home. Sleep has returned to a state of normalcy. The physical exam doesn't change other than to inform you of how great your baby is doing in growth and development.

What everyone hates about this appointment has to do with the immunizations. They really line them up for this visit, and no parent enjoys watching it happen. Imagine your baby looking at you after building months of trust and thinking you betrayed them. It's sad, but at least the two-month checkup comes and goes with the promise of zero three-month visits. Here's what you can expect your child to receive.

- HepB: If your baby didn't receive any of the two doses after birth or at the one-month appointment, they will receive one at this appointment.

- IPV vaccine (polio): The first dose happens at the two-month appointment, but expect to get more. Polio isn't a disease prevalent as much anymore, but that is mostly due to a vaccine being available.

- PCV vaccine (pneumococcal): Another vaccine that will be delivered multiple times. It helps fight infections that cause bacterial meningitis and pneumonia.

- DTaP vaccine (diphtheria, tetanus, and pertussis): DTaP will be given three times in the first year and then another two times by the age of six.

- RV vaccine (rotavirus): This oral vaccine avoids the needle pain that babies and parents hate about immunizations. But, be on the lookout for the symptoms that follow the medicine that your little one will take again. The tradeoff is vomiting and diarrhea.

- Hib vaccine (Haemophilus influenza type b.): This immunization fights infections that hit the joints, lungs, blood, ears, and skin. Your child will need two more doses later, but it's worth the pain since it helps avoid meningitis in kids under the age of five.

It's ideal that you and your significant other present a united front for the two-month appointment even if it's the only one you can manage to attend together. It's typical for the father to hold the baby while the mother uses her voice for encouragement. After the bandages are placed on the skin, you can pass your child over to their mother for some much needed comfort. Thankfully, another two months will pass before you have to bring your baby back for another checkup. Most medical professionals don't see the need for a three-month visit.

Care For the Father

The first three months have a lot of things going on at one time. It's a bit overwhelming for the strongest of guys. Don't listen to the fathers of the past who say it's time to man up and get your head in the game. Why? Well, they didn't do what you're doing. Back in the day, dads had the (unfortunate) luxury of playing daddy whenever it benefited their needs or time. This new brave world gives dads the opportunity to live life wholly as a family. It's an upgrade of the highest order, which is why you chose to be where you are right now. Don't let anyone guy-shame you into thinking you don't need to take on so much parental responsibility. They obviously haven't been lucky enough to experience such joy.

Now that you know the right decision was made, it's time to understand the cost of parenting. The cost isn't life-threatening in any way. It's not so hard that it pushes you to the brink of something you can't return from. Parenting a newborn is simply not easy, and it's exhausting.

Guys have a difficult time asking for and accepting help. You've been taught or trained that it's not the manly thing to do, but is drowning emotionally, mentally, or physically a manly thing? It's not. If someone is asking to help, it's because they want to help. It doesn't have to be something big. If you know your friend is at the store, it's okay to ask them to pick up formula or a few other essentials. Any moment where you don't have to leave the house while the baby is home is a win. Your inlaws might ask if they can watch the little one so you and your partner can get a break. Accept their offer. You don't have to send them away with the baby. Most parents find it difficult to let another person drive with their newborn, or you don't feel comfortable placing your child in someone else's house quite yet. You can easily say it's okay to watch the baby, but suggest that they do it at your house. The person/people will have everything at their disposal, your child is in a familiar environment, and you and your partner can go upstairs and get some valuable sleep.

Speaking of sleep. Don't try to stay up doing everything when your child and significant other are in slumberland. It makes sense to watch your show, clean, cook, or anything else when time allows for it, but you have to rest your eyes. Sleep when the baby sleeps, but also do what you can to help your little one sleep at the right time. They don't have a concept of night and day, so it's up to you to get their internal clock programmed to fit your ideal schedule.

You also need a connection to other people. A good way to feed your energy is to find parenting groups for new dads. As a new father, you are a part of an entire community of like-minded individuals, but you have to put forth an effort to see what it's all about. Scan the social media sites for new dad groups in your area. Find one that meets in person for coffee or something similar. Engage in conversation and ask each other questions that you wouldn't normally ask. If getting away is too problematic, then there are groups that meet online. You can search for one that has a group chat or meets virtually via Zoom or on a similar platform. If spirituality is something in your life, then try going to your church to see if potential life groups or small groups have something for dads. People need people, and you aren't excluded from that reality.

Chapter 8:

3–6 Months

Life with a newborn was something special. You spent hours staring at the little one smiling and making goofy faces. It seemed like your baby spent much of their time crying, but sleep was more common than you think. Newborns close their eyes between 14 and 16 hours per day, but waking up more often in between makes it seem like all any of you do is rest but you're never rested. You learned how to entertain, sit in silence, and distract your young one whenever they were wide awake. It was tiresome, but you wouldn't have traded it for anything in the world.

Say goodbye to that baby because the months have morphed them into a supercharged, engaged, bigger baby, and a loveable personality has joined them. They are becoming more aware of their surroundings and looking into exploring what they might've missed up until now. This new child fully knows they are in this world to stay, and they want to run things. Don't get scared. You're trading in the coos and simple joys of newborns for fast-paced excitement. In many ways, the ball of energy that makes up the three to six-month old stage is what a lot of parents had in mind when thoughts of babies entered their minds. Gear up, read up, and get ready for your new life… again.

By now, you know your child has grown familiar with recognizing voices that aren't there regularly. He or she doesn't only get quiet and fix their face to symbolize they understand the voice they hear isn't you or your partner. No, they recognize many of those other voices and know who is approaching them before they see the person. They stop what they're doing and make a little sound as if they are trying to let that person know they're right around the corner. This is all because their sense of perception is intensifying.

Have you ever watched an adult make a facial expression in public and a little kid does the exact same thing? Pay attention the next time you're in line at the grocery store or in a waiting area, and you will see an example. Well, that game of imitation starts when the child is in the three to six-month phase of life. It's exciting to know that you can put this book down and start making those faces with your baby. Instead of the kicking legs and swinging arms of joy, the response will be a younger version of you looking back. The developmental milestones at this stage are can't miss moments.

- Your baby will stay quiet while someone talks because they understand taking turns to speak
- Your baby begins to repeat sounds (typically sounds like mama and dada)
- They begin to laugh (laugh with them to encourage positive behavior. Record the moment and share it with the grandparents. There's nothing like a baby's laughter)
- Your baby finds themself in the mirror (this will entertain them for quite some time)

What to Do to Help

Although your sweet child is moving along quite well with development and growth, you can't forget how they reached this level. You and your significant other have been involved and doing this parenting thing as a team. Don't stop now. More and more things are going to catch your child's eyes. They notice you playing video games or their eyes seem to be more fixated on the television when it's playing something. As much as the world enjoys more television programming, it's a mistake to allow your child to become too engaged by that platform. This isn't to suggest that there aren't amazing shows for babies. Honestly, there are entire networks and streaming channels perfectly formatted to fit the needs of little ones for entertainment and education.

There isn't anything in this world that can replace the care, love, and attention that you and the mother provide for your baby. Picking up your child, talking to them, and playing with them is the greatest form of stimulation and education they can receive. You might think Sesame Street or similar programming gets the job done, but TV can't mimic the stimulation you would normally give. An awesome childcare facility would be a better option than network television. The facts are, babies have to have personal interaction to develop skills and to learn and understand language. Listening in on normal conversations at home will help increase language ability faster than plopping your child down to view an episode of Peppa Pig. Find an extra 10 minutes to read a baby book to your child. You'll be amazed at what it can do and how fast you'll notice changes in literacy skills.

This is the age when babies are more aware of their mouths, fingers, and toes. You might think babies put things in their mouths because that's what babies do. You wouldn't be wrong, but you would be missing the bigger picture. Much as you're reading the *New Dad Playbook to Win at Parenting* to gain a better perspective, your baby is placing that dog toy in their mouth for a similar reason. This isn't to poke fun at your kid. Instead, it's to explain that babies use their mouths to gain information. That's right, putting objects in their mouths is how they obtain information about said object. That also explains why the toes, feet, and fingers are usually the first things to enter through the mouth. So, get a handful of clean toys and let your baby go on an exploration of wonder. Place toys around them in their play area to encourage the use of their limbs to stretch and reach. These playful exercises will help strengthen muscles, further develop motor skills, improve hand and eye coordination, and get your baby more practice at rolling over.

More ways to help continuously increase development is by joining your child on the floor or near their play area. A good game of peek-a-boo is an easy and fun way to help develop object permanence and social skills. Object permanence is understanding that people and things continue to exist, even if a person cannot see, touch, or hear them. Did we just explain that whole "if a tree falls in the forest theory?" Using peek-a-boo for social learning teaches your baby that it's perfectly fine to take turns while playing. A good game of "give and take" is one of the earliest steps in getting your child ready for school. Many parents live by the mantra of sending their kids to school so teachers can teach, so they don't need to help. If you stay engaged in your child's life, they will be more than ready to succeed in life because learning starts now. It takes a village.

Let's see other ways peek-a-boo can help during the three to six-month range.

- Brain development: The game makes use of visual stimulation, which helps the baby develop new brain connections (synapses). It's all part of triggering learning behavior. If this skill never gets used, then the ability dies off.

- It strengthens the connection with older kids: Peek-a-boo is a game that gives instant feedback between the older child and baby. It's great if there's an older sibling or cousin in the family, or if the parents plan on having another baby later.

Each child develops at their own healthy rate. Parents need to understand that development cannot be forced. If a game like peek-a-boo or hiding around the corner brings a frightened look to your baby's face or no smile at all shows up, then disengage. It's a sign that your child isn't ready yet. Don't worry, they will join in when the time is right. Remember to focus on what you can do to help encourage your baby's can dos.

- Continue to place them in various positions to develop rolling and crawling skills while they adjust to controlling their body
- Develop daily routines while they adjust to their developing world
- Continue to offer new toys to help those exploring hands
- React to their reactions by using facial expressions, sounds, and actions
- Read to them so they can hear new words and learn familiar ones
- Sing to them

Sleep Training

One of the best things about your child getting more mature is enjoying nights where they actually sleep for hours and hours. It's coming, so get ready to enjoy it. Sleep training is when your baby learns to fall asleep without you. Yes, it's a game changer that all parents can't wait to experience. It works for babies who are ready to call it a night when bedtime is supposed to happen, and it's practical for those who still wake up in the middle of the night.

It's a milestone for sure, especially when your baby has gotten used to you going on infant rescue missions in the middle of the night. Acquiring the self-soothing skills for nightly resting is an option for all families, but knowing that each baby is different means it's going to happen at different moments for each child.

Whenever your child makes the adjustment, you shouldn't start sleep training until they are at least four months old. It's a crucial time in development because at this age, most babies are ready to stop the nightly feedings, they're old enough to self-soothe, and their internal sleep schedule has matured enough for their brains to relax late at night. Like with everything, there are outliers. Some babies can make the switch earlier than four months. Others might not be ready until they mature to six months. Don't let a slower process discourage you. Remember, each child is unique.

Like most methods, there isn't one specific way to train your child, so find the one that best fits what you and your significant other want to use. Some parents take parts from various techniques and join them together. There isn't one sure way of teaching sleep training to your little one. Here are a few popular methods.

- Pick the child up, put the child down: You comfort your child physically by picking them up in the night. That familiar touch is naturally soothing. The thing is, it also provides comfort to the parent who struggles to hear their child cry themselves to sleep. You risk holding your baby too long and getting them to expect you to continue to rescue them. The key is to pick them up, provide some moments of soothing, put them down, and leave the room.

- Ferber method (known as "check and console"): You gently put your baby in the crib when they are feeling tired. Say goodnight and leave the room. You know they're awake, so you check in on them in designated intervals. Don't pick them up. Look in on them and leave. Start out checking every 10 minutes. After a few times of doing that, then you can increase the time to 15 minutes, and then 20 minutes. You'll be able to judge how well this works for your baby. Some children enjoy seeing their parents' faces from time to time. It's similar to playing peek-a-boo. They know that you still exist when you're gone. It doesn't work for everyone.

- Cry it out (CIO): The name of the method speaks for itself. CIO is the go-to sleep training method for many parents. You place your baby in the crib while they're still awake. The hope is that they will develop the soothing technique that settles them down for the night. If they get upset, they'll cry it out and let sleep come to them. Prepare them with a light feeding and a dry diaper. The first few nights are when parents find out if they have what it takes to continue this method. Hearing your baby cry and cry isn't easy to do.

- The chair method: The chair method is similar to the Ferber method because you utilize time intervals again. Patience is a virtue for this one. Set a chair next to the crib and sit in it when you place your baby in the crib. After a specified time, you leave the room. You come back and do the same thing if they start to cry. The next night is the same, but you have to move the chair back a ways. The third night has you moving the chair back even more. The key is you have to stay seated until your child falls asleep each night.

- Bedtime fading: Here, you simply make adjustments to your child's bedtime. Pay attention to when your baby typically starts crying each night. If you put them to bed and the tears flow 20 minutes later, then that is their natural bedtime. You can adjust if you want an earlier time.

There's good news if you fear you're one of the parents who will have trouble hearing the cries at night. Sleep training takes about four nights to successfully pull it off. Longer or shorter times could have to do with the method of choice. Adjust the methods, pull from other methods, or change it up completely if you don't think one is a good fit. Feel confident in knowing that sleep training is extremely safe to use; however, if you see weeks go by without any positive results, you should contact your family doctor.

A white noise machine could also help with sleep training if you don't mind using it for longer sessions. A child might get used to having the quiet noise at night, and without it, they might suddenly start waking up at those inconvenient times again. The benefit of having a white noise machine is it mirrors the sound the baby heard in the womb. That soothing sway can relax the mind for hours. It also does a good job of drowning out the house sounds that might disturb your sleeping baby. Don't feel like you have to spend more money than you want to purchase the noisemaker. If you have an extra phone with wifi capability you can download a free app to use through the night. The Rain Sounds app is excellent and has plenty of choices to choose from. It's not exactly white noise, but some of the choices that might mimic the fan sound are the ocean rain, thunderstorm, rain on the roof, and rain on the sidewalk. You can go into the settings and make adjustments for each type of choice. Setting the wind higher, especially on the ocean, can create the sound needed to soothe your baby. There are also timers to set if you don't want the app running all night.

Rainy Mood is another option that works well. You can find it in the App Store or Google Play Store. They also have a desktop option if you want to check them out by visiting https://rainymood.com/.

Teething and Feeding

It's time to learn about the slobbering, drooling, painful process of teething. You'll notice teeth sprouting between four and six months of age. Look, your baby was born with those teeth hiding beneath the gum line, so it was only a matter of time before they made their presence known.

Look out for symptoms that your baby is teething. The drool will start pouring, and it will soak through the bib you tried using to catch it. Other signs include trouble sleeping, loss of appetite, frustration/irritability, loss of appetite, and being overly fussy. You're probably thinking, "I just got my baby on a sleep schedule." Yes, it's horrible because a teething baby is not feeling well. These symptoms are normal for any little one; however, there are a few signs to pay attention to that are red flags during teething such as diarrhea, fevers, and rashes.

There are ways to soothe your child when teething is too much to handle. Teething toys are great to buy. You can pick from this selection.

- Hard plastic and wooden rings
- Silicone animals
- Soft textured cloths
- Freezable teethers
- Mesh feeders

You will probably fall in love with mesh feeders. You can place frozen fruit and other items in them. Your baby's gums will be soothed while they're having a great snack packed with nutrients.

Those great teething snacks show you how much your baby has matured in the last three to six months of life. It's time to start introducing them to solids. The four to six-month period is the recommended schedule, but, of course, all babies hit milestones at their own pace. Don't start based on the months of age. Look for signs that indicate they are gearing up for a new adventure. If your child is sitting upright and supporting the weight of their head, you can get hopeful that the introduction to new flavors is upon your house. If you tried to give the kid soft food before (a lot of dads do this) and they quickly spit or vomited, then that was a natural sign of unreadiness. Babies have what's called tongue thrust reflex, which is the action of the tongue automatically pushing food out of the mouth to protect the baby, so don't feel bad if that happened to you. It was your little one's way of showing they weren't ready for solids. Try it now. If the tongue doesn't betray the mouth, then it could be time to make another introduction or two. If you are constantly eating around your baby, and now they make noises and follow your food around with their eyes, then it's their way of saying it's time to get started. If your wife or partner unloaded an entire day's ration of breastfeeding and the child is bellowing for more, then you don't need anymore signs. Give that baby some pureed goodness.

It's not time to eliminate the breast from the child's life. That remains their best option of obtaining nutrients. Get them used to the new schedule of mealtime, but stick with what they know first. Start the kid off with a regular meal of mother's milk, then do solids, and follow up with the milk again. That's the best way to get your baby used to the new way of living life. The day should end with milk or formula and start the same way for the next sunrise. Adjustments will have to be made based on how your child likes the milk to food ratio. There should be an understanding of how things go around the six-month mark. Put in a regular breakfast, lunch, and dinner menu to get your baby's meal clock wired properly.

The first food introductions are always the best. You get to see what your baby likes and loathes. The facial expressions are priceless, but the spitting of food onto you is less than desired. Your approach should be varied, and don't be afraid to go through everything to see what works and what doesn't. You never know, they may love those sweet potatoes. At four to six months you can go with enrichment grain cereal. Mixing a little with breast milk will give your baby's tongue a subtle hint of a familiar taste. Don't force too much in, and do expect to use the spoon to scoop up the globs that made it on the chin.

There will be moments of frustration for you and the child. Respect their choice to avoid your food. When it's time, they will eat. Gradually use less breast milk to create a thicker cereal.

Pureed foods such as fruits and vegetables come next. Sometimes tasting the food first is something the parents do to get the baby interested. Does it work? It's up in the air, but make sure you don't make a face when tasting the mashed peas. You don't want to scare them off. Giving a large sample size is a great way to introduce various amounts of cuisine to your baby early in life. Also, it's believed that an early introduction to foods known to cause allergies helps reduce the risk of developing food allergies later. You know adults and kids who have one or more allergies to peanuts, eggs, dairy, and gluten. You also knew kids who were picky eaters that grew into adults who are picky eaters. Maybe things would've been different with more pureed carrots, squash, or plums in their lives during the feeding exploration at four to six months of age.

Another way to encourage eating a variety of foods is to make your own baby foods. It's a doable task, and it doesn't cost too much money or time. What your baby consumes is determined by you and the mother. Mother's milk is already gold. Why not add to it by developing a baby menu of fresh and delicious flavors. A great thing about taking charge to prepare baby food is you know what's going into the batch, which means you can limit sugar, salt, and preservatives. You can keep the homemade food in the refrigerator for up to two days or you can freeze the baby food in freezer-safe containers for about three months. If you plan it correctly, you can prepare and cook two to three different batches. Keep enough from each meal plan to last those few days and freeze the rest. On the second day, make another two to three batches of different foods, and follow the same pattern. Your freezer can be stocked with enough baby food to allow more time for other things. It's a win if you choose to play the food game this way.

Take a look at some healthy choices to make for your baby. In most cases, you only need a blender to get started.

- Fresh or frozen blueberry puree with baby cereal (loaded with antioxidants)
- Avocado puree with lemon juice (healthy fats)
- Banana puree (use ripe bananas, easy to digest)
- Bean puree (pinto beans, black beans, or chickpeas with a little breastmilk)
- Butternut squash and apple puree
- Sweet potato puree

You have an opportunity to explore so many recipes and possibly come up with some concoctions that might surprise you. Add some extra sweetness to that spinach by mixing in some peaches. Sweet potato, breastmilk, whole milk yogurt, and bananas could turn into a great baby smoothie. Do brussel sprouts and strawberries really go together? The jury is out on that one but, hey, if you and your baby enjoy the mix, who are we to judge?

With everything positive, there is always something negative to look out for. Not all soft and solid foods are okay for your baby to have. Some parents don't check to make sure what's safe. The number one food that you might find given to babies that should always be avoided is honey. Many people grow to love nature's nectar, but it has to be avoided. If honey enters the child's system too soon, they can develop botulism due to the spores honey carries. Botulism is a poison caused by toxins that can create swelling, difficulty swallowing, and paralysis. Adults and older kids can move those spores out, but a baby can't. You'll probably hear the nurse give a reminder to avoid honey at an appointment, but it's good to know now. Raisins,

89

grapes, peanut butter, popcorn, and hot dogs are some other foods to avoid because your baby could choke. Always research new foods, or ask your midwife, before giving them to your child just to be safe.

The last thing to never give to your baby is cow's milk. There might be a desire to give cow's milk at a time when breast milk or baby formula is unavailable. You think warming it up will be okay and it will provide the nutrients needed. Well, be prepared to have your child projectile vomit all over you, themselves, the floor, the crib, the couch, and more. You wouldn't be the first dad to make that dreadful mistake, but reading this section should make it so that it won't happen. A baby's sensitive stomach can't handle the proteins in cow's milk. They are incapable of breaking it down, so they naturally toss it up. Why don't they stop drinking cow's milk after a few sips? One, they are hungry. Two, the flavor of warm cow's milk is pleasing. Three, you gave them the bottle when you were told not to attempt such a mistake.

Baby Proofing

Baby proofing is essential. Sure, the little guy isn't getting into much at first, and crawling doesn't typically start until nine months, but it's best to be ready. As soon as they can, they will crawl all over the place, including toward trouble. In fact, you can be sure that they will seek it out. Proofing your house is a must. Some things that need proofing seem a bit weird, but it's always better to be safe. Don't listen to the people who judge you and attempt to make fun of the measures you take to secure your house. They aren't you, and what you do for your family only needs to matter to your family.

Some of the weird proofing measures that you might not think about are house plants. Think about what could happen between a plant and your baby. You place your baby on their play mat, and things are going as expected. They're on their back looking at one of those plastic mirrors or it's tummy time and they're pushing back and forth making coos. The doorbell rings and you look to see it's a delivery person. In your mind, answering the door and taking the package only takes a few seconds. While at the door, you have to sign for the delivery. Meanwhile, your baby rolled over to the end table where a beautiful pot of Easter Lilies awaited. You were only gone for 50 seconds, but you returned to see the pot of Easter Lilies had been pulled down to the floor. The pretty colors were too much to ignore. The Easter Lily happens to be one of the more extreme toxic versions of the flower. All parts of the Easter Lily are toxic and shouldn't be ingested. Your child will be quick to put parts of the flower in their mouth. and then you have to call for help. Lilies happen to be flowers that people place in their house all of the time without realizing the potential danger to babies. Here's a list of plants to avoid or remove from your house.

- Lilies (Easter, Tiger, Asian, Day, Rubrum, Calla): the Calla Lily is fatal to children.
- Philodendron: causes swelling of the mouth and digestive tract.
- Pothos (Devil's Ivy): burns the mouth. Swells the tongue, lips, and throat. Causes diarrhea and vomiting.
- Arrowhead: Vomiting and skin irritation.
- Peace Lily (not a real Lily): swelling, vomiting, difficulties swallowing and speaking.
- Oleander: causes arrhythmia, vomiting, diarrhea. One leaf can kill an adult.

- Ivy (English Ivy): fever, rash, burning, and more.
- Mother-in-Law's Tongue (Snake Plant): low toxicity. Don't ingest.

You don't necessarily have to discard these plants, but you should use some safety measures. Hang the plants inside and out to keep children or pets from messing with them. Label the plants, and use gloves whenever dealing with toxic plants.

Pad the corners of your tables, entertainment console, chairs, and the corners in the living room, kitchen, bedroom, and more. Once your baby starts rolling around and flipping over, it's easy to move into something with a sharp edge. The older baby who pulls themselves up needs protection from those tables. Pretty much everything in your house is a disaster waiting to happen. It's the life you chose.

Babies love going into the kitchen to pull through those cabinets or get into the pet food. Cabinet locks will keep them from grabbing those pots and pans for their band of one. Another good reason is to protect them. The last thing you want is for a pot or pan to fall on their foot, or worse, hit them with force on top of their heads. The locks also keep the child from getting into the chemicals that adults place under sinks. It might make sense to place those items in the garage. Place the pet food into a storage container with tight snap-on lids or set it in the garage.

You need to purchase the plastic covers that push into the outlets. Babies enjoy finding small objects and pushing them into the open slots of the wall outlets. You'll risk electric shock to your child should anything happen.

Baby proof your savings. It makes sense to want to put extra money away to use for more important needs when the baby is born. Perhaps you're thinking of the future and turning your attention to investing. You still need items in the house to cover your child's needs and wants. Your mother-in-law says, "Don't waste your money on that $1,500 crib. I have one for you." The crib she has belonged to your girlfriend or wife's grandmother, and she's no longer with the family. Everyone's excited about this family heirloom. Here's some bad news for you... using that piece of furniture is a bad idea. Using hand-me-down cribs more than five years old might not meet safety requirements. Those older cribs were made with a drop-down side and, unfortunately, too many infant deaths were caused by those types of cribs. It's better to get something new and reliable.

Mount your bookshelves and entertainment centers to the walls. Babies don't stop moving once they figure out how to get going. A scooting or crawling little one will pull themselves up on different items. Sometimes that object falls forward as the baby pulls, and the child can't escape the pending doom. Secure your televisions as well. A baby will be more enthusiastic about reaching for that shiny TV with all of the pretty, moving pictures. It's a sad reality, but falling televisions have resulted in many infant deaths over the years.

Just like hand-me-down cribs, take a good look at those hand-me-down toys. Toys older than 10 years run the risk of material or paint chipping off, which is a bad thing for a baby placing that object in their mouth. Lead is also an issue in old toys. You might have that collection at your mother's house that you all played with as children, but don't allow your child to do the same. Another thing those decades-old toys come with are metal knobs to turn for wind-up toys. Those small pieces are sharp and hard. If your baby is playing with one and it falls on their face or head, it could cut them open. Older toys were also made with long cords. An excited baby rolling around could wrap that cord around their neck or other body parts.

Save yourself from walking into the kitchen to find a sea of refrigerator magnets. Your kid will surely pull them off and try to find other places to place them, like on your television. Plus, the backs of some magnets may easily be removed from a determined baby, which will turn the magnet strip into a choking hazard. Place the magnets up high on your refrigerator.

Get yourself a toilet lock as well. Little ones enjoy lifting that seat and seeing the extra water to play with. Occasionally, they find any type of item to shove down the flush hole. Other things to take care of are removing the extra plastic bags you have in your drawers. A good plastic bag turns into a helmet or face mask for mobilized children. They often get stuck inside of them, and the damage ends in suffocation. Getting a lock for your refrigerator will save you money and hours of cleaning up. Babies have been watching you or their mom in the kitchen opening and closing the doors of the refrigerator for months. It's their turn to pull themselves up and see what's inside. Eggs, milk, and anything else becomes part of the masterpiece your child spreads on the floor.

Also, place your batteries in a secure location. Babies love putting batteries in their mouth and sucking on them. Other hazards and proofing to look out for include the following.

- Twist ties for bread bags (choking, poking, and sticking)
- Pantry (cans, and opened food items)
- Loose keys
- Pen and pencil containers
- Cords (secure all cords behind furniture or similar)

Purchasing multiple baby gates will keep them from going up the stairs and into the kitchen when the time comes for them to sneak by you, and they will sneak by. To recap, here's a good list of items to buy to babyproof your house. This isn't the time to think about taking the cheap route. Your baby's safety is on the line.

- Cabinet locks
- Storage containers with snap in place lids
- Non-poisonous plants and plant hangers
- Corner protectors
- Plug socket covers
- Non-slip rug underlays
- Window restrictors and locks
- Baby gates
- Door stoppers
- Safety catches for cupboard doors and drawers
- Anti-tip straps or brackets for heavy furniture
- Toilet lid locks

Budgeting for New Times

How do you handle the changes in your financial life now that the baby has been home? You're finding that the cost is a bit more than you expected. Not just the cost of taking care of your child, but medical expenses as well. Let's say your insurance is good. A lot of items were covered, but unless you're a military member, the complete cost didn't get handled by insurance. With reliable health insurance, the cost out of pocket could still total close to $7,000 in the United States, which isn't known for the best healthcare system. The amounts increase drastically for vaginal and Cesarean without the proper coverage. You're looking at over $13,000 and $22,000 respectively.

What's the plan to take care of those bills? Ignoring them isn't an option and you still have a family to take care of.

Another scenario is if your partner hasn't gone back to work. Sometimes you decide together that she's going to stay home and be a mother or a housewife. Perhaps, she isn't ready physically or emotionally to return after having a baby. It's time to figure things out because life isn't going to get cheaper.

One thing you can do is start budgeting if you haven't already. There are financial advisors, apps, and other ways to figure out where to start. First, you need to know how much money is coming in compared to how much is going out. You went from a two-income, two-person family to a one-income, three-person family. Already, the math doesn't add up! Start gathering the information.

- Rent/Mortgage
- Car loan payments
- Health insurance: one or two policies
- Car insurance: one or two policies
- Auto gas/petrol
- Utilities: electric, gas, water, trash disposal, and any taxes
- Lawncare
- Internet
- Cellular service

- Cable/streaming service: nowadays this adds up. You have Netflix, Disney+, Hulu, HBOMax, Peacock, Starz, Showtime, ESPN+, and more.
- Student loans
- Coffee shop
- Groceries
- Pet care

There's no telling how much you'll find when you start adding things up. Those streaming services can get out of hand very quickly. We live in a world where we sign up for free trials, but then we forget to cancel them. A possible $7.99/month doesn't seem like a lot until you multiply that by twelve.

For the first six months, it can cost anywhere from $6000 to $7000 to take care of your baby. It's essential to find the best budgeting tool you can. One recommendation is to utilize Financial Peace University by Dave Ramsey. This method helps you utilize a complete budget every month. Dave also tries to have you use cash for everything and takes you through "seven baby steps" to zero in on eliminating debt and maximizing your savings. The first step is to have $1,000 in an emergency fund, then you work on paying off debt utilizing a tool called "debt snowball." Here is a link to learn more. https://www.businessinsider.com/personal-finance/dave-ramsey-financial-peace-university-what-you-learn

Like with most things, there isn't a surefire way to budget, and the method you pick doesn't necessarily mean you have to use all of its steps. Sit down with your partner and decide what's best for your family. One thing you know for sure is, taking care of the baby isn't going to get cheaper.

Some other tips include finding ways your partner can earn income on the side while staying at home with the child. Social media is a great way to look into those options. There are groups of people who have set up pages to help network with others.

Conclusion

There is a lot to take in when you're preparing to be a first-time father. Once again, you came to the right place. Be proud of yourself for understanding that you weren't ready for the mysteries surrounding pregnancy and childbirth. Listen to the people who offer you encouragement and advice when it comes to taking on the unbelievable journey of fatherhood. It's great to have a community of people to lean on when your new life gets to be more than you can comprehend or handle; however, remember that what you and your partner will experience will be much different than every other person you come across or who gives you details on what to expect. You might share similarities, but your child is uniquely created to be special to your family.

You accomplished a lot of firsts from the moment you found out about the pregnancy to hitting the six-month mark with your child. How did you manage to hold it all together? Oh, that's right, you prepped and read and did it all over again to be sure. Many dads are there, but not all of them show up. You have proven that showing up means taking charge of the people in your life. Not control, but taking on the responsibility for their health and safety. Could you imagine being the type of guy a baby could depend on when you first picked up the *New Dad Playbook to Win at Parenting*? But you did it. Your child knows what it's like to have a father in their life. It's the kind of feeling that makes you appreciate the life you've been given and the life you continue to mold.

Some of you finished reading this book and you haven't hit any of the childbirth milestones. Others are checking off those monumental moments at this very moment. Wherever you are right now, know that every dad who is doing the right thing is proud of you. You are the kind of man worth remembering. You don't understand that purchasing this book, reading the contents, and sharing the information is helping to usher in new generations of dads who will not only know what it's like to be a father but understand how to win at parenting. You also became part of one big dad network and support system. You're not alone in this journey, and it's essential to memorize those words and tattoo them on your head. Any lost dad has a chance at being found and turning their entire perspective on its rear end.

It must feel amazing to sit down with your partner or spouse and happily share what you know your life will be now that you've taken the plunge into discovering who you want to be as a father and husband/partner. What have they said to you about the new man you've become? Hopefully, she's ecstatic and can't wait to either complete this process with you or start a new one with another little goal waiting to meet the world.

You can prepare to take on the role of father with confidence. The decision you made to be where you are to support and raise your family is one of significant importance. You don't have to have all of the tools to step into the world of dad right now, but the *New Dad Playbook to Win at Parenting* has given you a blueprint to follow and go back to when more guidance is necessary. Don't be afraid to take this to the stores when you're making moves to improve your house. Feel brave enough to carry it with you to doctor appointments and into the labor and delivery room. Trust that the OB/GYN or midwife will be impressed by the quality of questions you ask pertaining to the pregnancy.

Some things are going to change as time goes by. Reading this handbook once isn't enough to make you an expert, so read it again and again. Give other fathers advice, but tell them, "Hey, purchase the *New Dad Playbook to Win at Parenting*" if true parenting success is what they desire. You should feel more than ready to take the next step in this parenting adventure. We want you to succeed and be the best dad that your little boy or precious girl deserves. We want you prepared to share this new life with your partner, and help her feel secure in who she is preparing to become. This guide is perfect for bridging the gap of the next nine months into the first six months of your child's life. There's a lot to unpack, and much to wonder about.

There are many men who are reading this or who have finished the book, but we can reach more. We live in a time when grandparents have taken on the role of the parent while their kids fail to step up to life's responsibility. Raising their kids into adulthood doesn't mean they should avoid this book. A grandfather doesn't understand how to raise a child in the digital age. We have a lot to teach them, so send them over to read the material that will guide them to becoming second-dad with class. The grandfathers can shed that old-school approach to being a guy and start learning what it takes to be a dad.

The thing about being a father is, all of the things that we struggle with… the reasons why this book was created, only matter to us. Our babies grow up, and they only remember that we were there. They can say they had a dad who chose to stick around. He chose to be there when it mattered, and for them, that's all that matters.

But wait, parenting doesn't stop where this book leaves off. How are you going to handle raising your child from six months to two years (the terrible twos)? We didn't prepare you for such an adventure. You and the future fathers-to-be will have to come back and read the next installment: *How to Win at Parenting—from Birth to Two Years*.

References

Acosta, K. (2021, July 22). *Best pregnancy apps for 2021*. Forbes health. https://www.forbes.com/health/family/best-pregnancy-apps/

Are birth classes covered by insurance? (2021, April 29). Motherly. https://www.mother.ly/life/birth-classes-covered-by-insurance/

Australia, H. (2021, August 15). *Sleep during pregnancy*. Pregnancybirthandbaby. https://www.pregnancybirthbaby.org.au/sleep-during-pregnancy

Ben-Joseph, E. P. (2018). *Breastfeeding vs. formula feeding (for parents)*. Kidshealth. https://kidshealth.org/en/parents/breast-bottle-feeding.html

Birth doula and childbirth educator training and certification with birthing from within. (n.d.). Birthing from within. https://birthingfromwithin.com/

Bradley, S. (2021, March 16). *Everything you need for your baby: 3_6 months*. Verywell family. https://www.verywellfamily.com/everything-you-need-for-your-baby-3-to-6-months-4845886

Cassata, C. (2020, January 10). *Here's what happens to your body when you cut out alcohol for 30 days*. Healthline. https://www.healthline.com/health-news/what-happens-to-your-body-when-you-quit-alcohol-for-30-days

Cassell, A. (2021). *A childbirth cheat sheet for dads-to-be*. BabyCenter. https://www.babycenter.com/pregnancy/relationships/a-childbirth-cheat-sheet-for-dads-to-be_8244

CDC. (2018). *Important milestones: Your baby by six months*. Centers for Disease Control and Prevention. https://www.cdc.gov/ncbddd/actearly/milestones/milestones-6mo.html

CDC. (2020, February 25). *Baby vaccines at birth*. Centers for Disease Control and Prevention. https://www.cdc.gov/vaccines/parents/by-age/newborn-birth.html

Charmaine. (2017, July 18). *10 Remedies for morning sickness*. Facty health. https://facty.com/conditions/pregnancy/10-remedies-for-morning-sickness/1/

Coleman, P. A. (2017, October 2). *The new dad's ultimate strategy guide for surviving your baby's first month*. Fatherly. https://www.fatherly.com/parenting/new-dad-survival-tips-first-month/

Colleen, de Bellefonds. (2014, October 6). *10 Signs of labor*. What to expect. https://www.whattoexpect.com/pregnancy/labor-signs

Cronkleton, E. (2020, August 7). *The best stretch mark creams for pregnancy*. Healthline. https://www.healthline.com/health/pregnancy/best-stretch-mark-creams-for-pregnancy#our-picks

Default - stanford children's health. (2019). Stanfordchildrens.org. https://www.stanfordchildrens.org/en/topic/default?id=first-trimester-85-P01218

Dunn, L. (2019, October 4). *I took one of financial guru dave ramsey's most popular courses to get better with money, and i'm happy to say it's working.* Business insider. https://www.businessinsider.com/personal-finance/dave-ramsey-financial-peace-university-what-you-learn

Emotional and social development: birth to 3 months. (2021, April 2). Healthychildren. https://www.healthychildren.org/English/ages-stages/baby/Pages/Emotional-and-Social-Development-Birth-to-3-Months.aspx

familydoctor.org editorial staff. (2009, October). *Changes in your body during pregnancy: second trimester.* Familydoctor. https://familydoctor.org/changes-in-your-body-during-pregnancy-second-trimester/

4 Types of childbirth classes you should know about. (n.d.). Kindred bravely. https://www.kindredbravely.com/blogs/bravely/childbirth-classes-you-should-know

Gorin, A. (2021, March 29). *The complete guide to starting baby on solids.* Parents. https://www.parents.com/baby/feeding/solid-foods/starting-solids-guide/

Gregory, C. R. (n.d.). *Labor tips for first time moms.* Parents. https://www.parents.com/pregnancy/giving-birth/labor-and-delivery/6-delivery-day-jitters/

105

Grunebaum, A. (2020, June 14). *Can dreams reveal pregnancy before a home pregnancy test?* BabyMed. https://www.babymed.com/can-dreams-reveal-a-pregnancy-before-the-home-pregnancy-test#

Hospital bag checklist—what to pack. (2021, November 21). Pampers. https://www.pampers.com/en-us/pregnancy/giving-birth/article/what-to-pack-in-your-hospital-bag-go-bag-checklist

Ipatenco, S. (2017, June 13). *Can eating too much protein be dangerous while pregnant?* Hello motherhood. https://www.hellomotherhood.com/article/547795-can-eating-too-much-protein-be-dangerous-while-pregnant/

Kendra Cherry. (2019). *Important milestones of cognitive development in children.* Verywell mind. https://www.verywellmind.com/cognitive-developmental-milestones-2795109

Kinsey, J. (2022, February 24). *10 Toxic houseplants that are dangerous for children and pets.* Dengarden. https://dengarden.com/gardening/Dangerous-Beauties-Twenty-Toxic-Houseplants-to-Avoid-Around-Children-and-Pets

Marcin, A. (2018, December 6). *When is the best time to announce pregnancy?* Healthline. https://www.healthline.com/health/pregnancy/when-to-announce-your-pregnancy#risk-of-miscarriage

Mayo Clinic. (2017). *Fetal development: what happens during the 3rd Trimester?* Mayo clinic. https://www.mayoclinic.org/healthy-lifestyle/pregnancy-week-by-week/in-depth/fetal-development/art-20045997

Miles, K. (2021). *The lamaze method of childbirth* Babycenter. https://www.babycenter.com/pregnancy/your-body/the-lamaze-method-of-childbirth_640

Monthly breakdown of your child's biggest expenses. (n.d.). Newyorklife. https://www.newyorklife.com/articles/breakdown-of-biggest-expenses-for-your-child

Morning sickness, nausea & vomiting of pregnancy. (2017, June 29). Cleveland clinic. https://my.clevelandclinic.org/health/diseases/16566-morning-sickness-nausea-and-vomiting-of-pregnancy

Newman, T. (2021, July 29). *Pregnancy diet: what to eat and what to avoid.* Medicalnewstoday. https://www.medicalnewstoday.com/articles/246404#guidelines

Oakley, C. (2014, July 21). *Ready to get pregnant? Dad's health matters.* Webmd. https://www.webmd.com/baby/features/pregnancy-dad-health

October 21, B. L. U., & 2019. (2019, October 21). *Family planning conversations to have before becoming parents.* Real simple. https://www.realsimple.com/work-life/family/starting-a-family

Palanjian, A. (2020, January 22). *10 Easy homemade baby food ideas (no-cook, super fast, stage 1).* Yummy toddler food. https://www.yummytoddlerfood.com/homemade-baby-food/

Pathways. (2015). Pathways. https://pathways.org/

Peek a boo. (2017, July 12). Parent trust for Washington children. https://www.parenttrust.org/for-families/parenting-advice/parentingtips/early-learning/peek-a-boo/

Pegden, C. (2016, November 8). *20 Week anatomy + anomaly pregnancy scan*. The medical chambers. https://www.themedicalchambers.com/specialties/ultrasound/20-week-pregnancy-scan

Prager, S. (2021, July 21). *When should a baby sleep in their own room? The best time to make the switch*. NewFolks. https://www.newfolks.com/inspiration/baby-sleep-own-room/

Pregnancy, sex drive and your relationship: for women. (2022, February 23). Raising children network. https://raisingchildren.net.au/pregnancy/preparing-for-a-baby/relationships/pregnancy-sex-drive-your-relationship-women

Pullano, N. (2020, January 14). *When babies make eye contact and what to expect as their eyes develop over the first year of life*. Insider. https://www.insider.com/when-do-babies-make-eye-contact

Robock, K. (2017, May 16). *3 Tips for surviving the first three months with baby*. Today's parent. https://www.todaysparent.com/pregnancy/3-tips-for-surviving-the-first-three-months-with-baby/

Sassos, S., MS, RDN, CSO, CDN, NASM-CPT, & Institute, G. H. (2021, July 22). *15 Best pregnancy exercises by trimester, according to experts*. Good housekeeping.

https://www.goodhousekeeping.com/health/fitness/a37050658/pregnancy-exercises/

Second-hand smoke and third-hand smoke: effects on children. (2021, March 30). Raising children network. https://raisingchildren.net.au/babies/health-daily-care/health-concerns/second-hand-smoke

Seitz, J. (2017, July 18). *The importance of skin-to-skin with baby after delivery.* Sanford health. https://news.sanfordhealth.org/childrens/the-importance-of-skin-to-skin-after-delivery-you-should-know/

Shaziya Allarakha, MD. (2022, January 21). *Are pacifiers good or bad for newborns?* Medicinenet. https://www.medicinenet.com/are_pacifiers_good_or_bad/article.htm

Sweeney, M. (2017, April 27). *12 Best changing tables (2022 reviews).* Mom loves best. https://momlovesbest.com/diapering/changing-tables#:~:text=Price%3A%20Changing%20tables%20can%20range

Taylor, M. (2020, May 21). *The 5 Best drinks for pregnant women _ plus beverages to avoid.* What to expect. https://www.whattoexpect.com/pregnancy/eating-well/what-to-drink-during-pregnancy.aspx

Teen, L. (2019, July 18). *Newborn checkup schedule for month 0-4 (All of your questions covered!).* Mommy labor nurse. https://mommylabornurse.com/newborn-checkup schedule/

Teething signs and symptoms - american dental association. (n.d.). Mouthhealthy. https://www.mouthhealthy.org/en/az-topics/t/teething

Tepper, T. (2020, April 15). A simple trick to reset your post-baby budget. *The New York times*. https://www.nytimes.com/2020/04/15/parenting/new-baby-budget.html

Terreri, C. (2018, October 8). *How early can you tell if you're pregnant?* Lamaze international. https://www.lamaze.org/Giving-Birth-with-Confidence/GBWC-Post/how-early-can-you-tell-if-youre-pregnant

Tobah, Y. (2020, August 18). *Headaches during pregnancy: what's the best treatment?* Mayo clinic. https://www.mayoclinic.org/healthy-lifestyle/pregnancy-week-by-week/expert-answers/headaches-during-pregnancy/faq-20058265

Webb, C. (2021, January 18). *Top 11 Healthy food chefs on social media in 2022*. Websta. https://websta.me/healthy-food-chefs-on-social-media/

Website. (n.d.). *Preeclampsia - signs-and-symptoms*. Preeclampsia. https://preeclampsia.org/signs-and-symptoms?gclid=Cj0KCQiA95aRBhCsARIsAC2xvfwYDSwsi3uMxJDBSkiwBQ5-L3_uwg-7kARNDEV2Gbx8rwmZe1PeKRQaArmBEALw_wcB

What is hypnobirthing? (n.d.). Hypnobirthing. https://us.hypnobirthing.com/about/what-is-hypnobirthing-definition/

When and how to sleep train your baby. (2021, May 3). Cleveland clinic. https://health.clevelandclinic.org/when-and-how-to-sleep-train-your-baby/

When to start buying baby stuff + must-have items for pregnancy. (2021, July 2). The postpartum party. https://thepostpartumparty.com/when-to-start-buying-baby-stuff/

Wisner, W. (2022, January 12). *Your 3-Month-old baby's development & milestones.* Verywell family. https://www.verywellfamily.com/your-3-month-old-baby-development-and-milestones-4172049

Printed in Great Britain
by Amazon